MOLIÈRE
TARTUFFE

MOLIÈRE
TARTUFFE

MOLIÈRE
TARTUFFE

A perfect mix of hilarity
and scathing satire--
the master stroke
of theatre's master comedian.

EURIPIDES
THE TROJAN WOMEN

A tragedy of unequaled insight
into the ravages of war
from the point of view
of the daughters and wives
of the vanquished.

WILLIAM SHAKESPEARE
AS YOU LIKE IT

A romantic enchantment,
peopled with some of Shakespeare's
most endearing creations.

HENRIK IBSEN
GHOSTS

A gripping drama
that pits respectability
against allegiance
to a deeper obligation.

ANTON CHEKHOV
CHEKHOV VERY FUNNY

An evening of the most farcical sketches ever played,
including "Concerning the Injuriousness of Tobacco,"
"The Bear," "The Marriage Proposal,"
and "Swan Song."

20/20 Is Not Enough: The New World of Vision (1990)
(with Drs. Arthur Seiderman and Steven Marcus)

Monte Cassino (1984)
(with David Richardson)

The Murder of Napoleon (1982)
(with Ben Weider)

The Average Man Fights Back (1977)

The Screwing of the Average Man (1974)

Tender Loving Greed (1974)
(with Mary Adelaide Mendelson)

Diplomaism (1971)

Agents of Change: A Close Look at the Peace Corps (1968)
(with Meridan Bennett)

*No Easy Harvest: The Dilemma of Agriculture in
Underdeveloped Countries (1967)*
(with Max F. Millikan)

Africa (1965)
(Your World in Focus series)

Africa from Independence to Tomorrow (1965)

TRANSLATIONS

The Totalitarian Temptation (1977)
by Jean-François Revel

My Father's House (1951)
by Henri Troyat

Year of the Pearl

YEAR
OF THE
PEARL

The Life of a New York Repertory Company

DAVID HAPGOOD

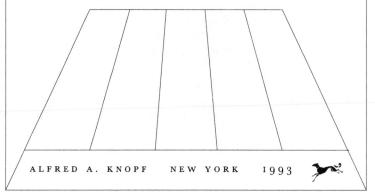

ALFRED A. KNOPF   NEW YORK   1993

THIS IS A BORZOI BOOK
PUBLISHED BY ALFRED A. KNOPF, INC.

Grateful acknowledgment is made to New American Library for permission to
reprint excerpts from *Tartuffe* from *Tartuffe and Other Plays* by Molière, translated
by Donald M. Frame, translation copyright © 1967 by Donald M. Frame.
Reprinted by permission of New American Library, a division of Penguin Books
U.S.A., Inc.

Library of Congress Cataloging-in-Publication Data
Hapgood, David.
Year of the Pearl : the life of a New York repertory
company / by David Hapgood. — 1st ed.
p.   cm.
ISBN 0-679-41165-8
1. Pearl Theatre (New York, N.Y.)   2. Theater—United
States—New York—History—20th century.   I. Title.
PN2297.P35H57   1993
792'.09747'1—dc20   93-20246   CIP

Manufactured in the United States of America

FIRST EDITION

For Janice

Year of the Pearl

Shepard Sobel arrives at the theatre about 6:30 this morning. He's almost always the first one here, and today he's earlier than usual: this will be one of the most important days of his forty-four years. It is the first day of the theatre's make-or-break season. In the next eight months, Sobel will—or he will not—take a giant step toward realizing the dream he had in mind when he founded the Pearl seven years ago.

From the outside the Pearl Theatre doesn't look like anyone's dream house. Its two-story home on a gritty side street in the West Twenties of Manhattan is overshadowed by huge, gloomy warehouse and office-furniture buildings. Since the Pearl company moved in, another small theatre has settled on the block, but it's still the kind of street where you'd sooner expect to encounter moving men than members of Actors' Equity. As you walk along the street from Sixth Avenue on this steaming summer morning, a handful of derelicts are lying around on the warehouse landing; should you come from the other direction, you'll pass their counterparts, ravaged-looking men sitting quiet as turtles on the steps of a halfway house. When you reach the Pearl, nothing about the exterior says theatre: in fact its concrete front, painted blood-red trimmed with a garish blue, doesn't say anything at all.

Everything you find inside is small in scale. You enter directly into a tiny lobby that can accommodate no more than two dozen people. The wall at left is covered with photos of the Pearl's actors in productions going back seven seasons. At right is the ladder that the stage manager and the lighting operator use to climb through a hole in the ceiling to their duty posts. You go up five steps to enter the theatre itself. It has seventy-two seats, arranged in eight rows; the Pearl, unlike many small theatres, is well raked—that is, slanted—for visibility, and the blue plush seats are comfortably padded. Almost everything you see is black: the stage, the walls, the ceiling. The twenty-foot-wide stage accommodates only minimal sets. There is no curtain. A corridor backstage leads to the two dressing rooms. Out back, to my surprise, is a small yard with a few plants.

Sobel, an actor and sometime English teacher, launched the Pearl Theatre in 1984 "on half a shoestring" and has been its artistic director ever since. He'd been knocking around the theatre off and on since his college days, acting and directing without notable success, and he'd come to believe the only way he could do what he wanted was with a theatre of his own. He'd found the compelling purpose of his life: his theatre soon absorbed virtually all his waking hours except the few he had to give to earning a meager living. He gave the theatre its name because "a pearl is a living thing that grows slowly. It's round but not perfect, it's rough at the edges. It needs human contact to make it beautiful. I like the thought that a pearl grows from a grain of sand that is an irritation to the oyster." The pearl's slow growth suggests the theatre's debt to generations past, and also Sobel's debt to his own ancestors: his mother's name is Pearl. Sobel advertised in the *Dramatists Guild Quarterly* for plays to stage, and in the same issue he offered his services to type scripts: "I was a producer and a typist." It hasn't changed so very much. Until two years ago, Sobel was typing (medical research papers by then) from 6:30 to 8:30 every morning, before going twenty blocks downtown to the Pearl, where he would stay till he closed the building after the evening performance. The Pearl couldn't afford health insurance, so when Sobel needed surgery not long ago, he flew to Colorado, where his surgeon brother had arranged for a free operation; the flight was paid for with his other brother's frequent-flier credits. His salary in 1990–91 was $9,600.

By the second season Sobel had decided he wanted his Pearl to have a resident acting company that would stage plays from the classics of Western theatre. The classics, because that's what New York was lacking. "If you're designing a building, you want to add to the skyline," Sobel says. (He likes to talk in metaphors, which is as it should be, considering that theatre itself is a metaphor: fictional people through whom we learn the truth about real people.) He wanted a resident company, because only actors who are trained for the classics in voice and movement and who work together from show to show can do justice to the plays they perform. That continuing experience was what would give the Pearl's playing of the classics its unique value; that was what he would add to the skyline of theatre in New York. The company would be an ensemble without stars; the actor who played Hamlet one time might be a gravedigger next.

In its seven years, the Pearl has built a reputation for its uncompromising fidelity to the playwrights whose works it performs. "We try to take the audience to the playwright, not the playwright to the twentieth century" is how Sobel puts it: no modern-dress Shakespeare, or Oedipus in Abilene. But in the economics of New York theatre, the price of survival has been that all the Pearl's members have had to work at other jobs, even during the run of a show, in order to keep themselves alive and the theatre open. (During the 1990–91 season each actor was paid a total of $750 for the seven weeks of a show's run.) They paint apartments, work as Kelly stenographers, type legal papers, teach acting and voice, and when they're lucky they do a television commercial or a day or two on a soap opera; against all expectations, not one Pearl actor waits tables in a restaurant. Yet as actors they are all highly skilled and well regarded in their profession.

Now the Pearl family—Sobel and the actors, joined by their board of trustees—has decided on a daring attempt to move to a different theatrical level. To achieve that goal, the Pearl has to almost double both its budget and its audience—in one season. A risky move in a bleak time, but one that would bring the Pearl a long step closer to the theatre Sobel sees in his dreams.

It was the Pearl's reputation that first brought me to West Twenty-second Street, but the story begins many years before. I was five years old. A big man with white hair was visiting us. He spoke to my mother in a strange language, but to me he spoke in a way any child would understand. He put on a private show for me. For his makeup, he hung my mother's handbag from his chin to make a beard and he clipped clothespins to his upper lip for a moustache. In one snapshot, with pince-nez and a clothespin on his nose, he looks a little like Woodrow Wilson. I remember his booming laughter at my delighted response to his performance. Of course I was delighted. The performer was Constantin Stanislavski.

My mother was Stanislavski's translator, and they were together to work on what would five years later be published as *An Actor Prepares*, the first statement of his revolutionary beliefs about the art of acting. Stanislavski and his theatre became the centerpiece of my mother's professional life, and an important part of her personal life as well. In the years of my growing up, actors from the Moscow Art Theatre, living in exile in New York, were often guests at our apartment. To me they were fabulous beings. They'd change identities at the drop of a hint, and each new self they assumed was so brightly colored the rest of us seemed in monotone by comparison. They made us laugh and, because they were exiles, they cried a lot too.

Decades hurried by. I have always kept my love of live performance and my child's wonder at the actors who bring other people to life for us: it is the most direct and amazing of the arts. I've been fortunate to live in a city that is rich in theatre. In too many communities, theatre has been completely replaced by movies and television. Actors and audience can no longer meet in that extraordinary communion across the footlights—there's a screen between us. It's a tragic loss of an ancient and uniquely valuable part of our lives.

New York, however, is still the undisputed capital of theatre in America. It is the magnet that draws aspiring actors from every corner of the nation, the mythic place where the competition is fiercest and the standards highest, the arena in which you must test yourself against the best if you are to be taken seriously in the world of live performance. Among New York theatres, the best-known, of course, are the big commercial houses of Broadway that live by their receipts at the box office. But there's also another world of theatre here, which, measured by the size of its audience, is equal to Broadway. Here is where my wife and I spend most of our theatre evenings, and it's where we've had our most exciting theatrical experiences: those moments between actors and audience that make live theatre so passionate an art. This world consists of about 150 small theatres: the number changes every year as some die and others are born; sadly, it has been shrinking since recession gripped the city in the late 1980s. These theatres do not and cannot support themselves entirely on their ticket sales. The gap has to be filled by contributions from one source or another. I'd come to be particularly aware of the size of that gap, and the difficulty of filling it, since I became a trustee of a small foundation whose goal is to help preserve just such small theatres.

I'd been wanting for years to write about one of these small nonprofit theatres that have meant so much to us and that are as distinctive a part of New York's landscape as the money-crazed alleys of Wall Street. I wanted to seek out the human story behind a single theatre by living through a season with the people who make it possible. What is this life like? What kind of people live it and what do they get out of it? Most of all, I wondered, what reward do they get that compensates for the sacrifices they make? The Pearl struck me as a good place to seek the answers. We'd seen a number of sparkling performances behind the garish blue shell of the Pearl's facade. Theatre at its best transforms us; and several of our transforming experiences had taken place at the Pearl. We liked seeing the classics done straightforwardly, and we'd admired the simple effectiveness of the sets and costumes we saw on that tiny stage. We'd noticed the quiet competence of its management. I was intrigued by the courage it must take to try to grow while similar theatres were shrinking and disappearing. I'd come to know Shepard Sobel, and I thought he would be an excellent guide and companion on my journey of discovery.

Sobel is a native New Yorker who has spent most of his working life in the theatre. (He pronounces his name SO-bel, not so-BEL.) The person you meet contradicts the images those facts suggest. New Yorkers are supposed to be brash if not rude, but Sobel is the unusually courteous person who, when he phones, first asks if it's convenient for you to talk to him. Theatre people all too often talk in stagy exaggeration; Sobel's manner is low-keyed and modest. Ask him about his past, and he will speak of his "very unsuccessful acting career." His soft-spoken intelligence, his eloquent expression of his thoughts, would be rare in any field. This attractive man of medium build, whose curly black hair is just beginning to gray in his mid-forties, is a missionary who gives his waking life to the Pearl—and never raises his voice either to preach or to rebuke. As I soon learned, the inner man is austere and unwavering in his principles, both artistic and ethical; but what you meet is a good-natured soul with a lively sense of humor, one who will not easily let himself be topped in an exchange of wisecracks: a missionary who can poke fun at himself.

When I arrive at eight o'clock on this August morning that begins the new season, Sobel is checking the paper supply in the Pearl's two bathrooms. (As every Pearl fan knows, one of the theatre's distinctive attributes is that the bathrooms take up space that should be part of the stage, so that the set has to be planned around them. They cannot be used during performance; the minimum length of an intermission at the Pearl can be defined by how long it takes the audience to use the bathrooms.) "One of the duties of an artistic director," Sobel says with a smile, showing me the roll of paper in his hand. He's dressed for it, in faded blue jeans, black T-shirt, and paint-streaked sneakers.

I help him collect chairs—sixteen of them—from various of the theatre's nooks and crannies; most of the chairs are battle-scarred and some are patched with tape. We set the chairs on the bare stage around a big table, put together from several smaller ones. Sobel and an unseen person up in the booth above and behind the seats are testing the lights that hang in rows from the ceiling. Sobel can't get the effect he wants, soft lighting "so people won't feel they're on stage," and at the same time a good light for reading. "You'd think I'd know how to do this," Sobel says ruefully. "Well, what are the other choices?" He remains calm, and the lighting crisis is soon solved. A few minutes later he is on the phone calling a plumber about a leak in the clothes washer.

In the Pearl's backyard I find actress Joanne Camp, watering the few flowers. I'd met Camp on my first visit to discuss my project with Sobel. He'd suggested I talk with one of the actors, and I remembered Camp from her powerful performance two seasons earlier as Medea. She is a tall, handsome woman of forty with sharp features and long reddish-blond hair; her large green eyes are marvelously expressive. She does not look anything like the dark Medea in my mind's eye, but I'd found Camp's portrayal completely convincing. I recalled especially her flashing eyes when her Medea stared at Jason across the wreckage of their crimes. The night we met, we went after the show to a Seventh Avenue bar and grill. In our conversation there, Camp introduced me to the frustrations of serious acting. Medea is of course one of the very greatest roles for an actress. Audiences loved Camp's Medea, critics praised it, but she was never satisfied. "I never got it right, I never got enough hate, and I was terrified every night when I went on stage," she recalled. "Acting requires everything you can give, and sometimes—only sometimes—it gives you something back. Sometimes you come out empty-handed. That's what happened to me with Medea. So one year I'd like to do it again." Sobel, discussing *Medea* in his annual report, made the point in his own distinctive manner: "Greek tragedy, like all really great plays, must only ever be tackled for the second time—never the first." Sometime during that first evening I learned that Sobel and Camp are husband and wife. Now, in the yard, I chat briefly with Camp about her part in the current production, and then it is time to go inside.

The other actors start straggling in around ten, half an hour before the rehearsal is called. On an August day, most are in shorts or jeans; the only skirt I see is worn by the only actress who is past fifty. A young blonde in biking shorts skates up on roller blades. The actors exchange greetings and embraces. Most of them know each other. Four are members of the Pearl company, another is a former member. Of the six others, two are apprentices, one has worked here before, and three are appearing at the Pearl for the first time. Many of the actors have met on one stage or another in the relatively small world of live theatre. The apprentices are in their twenties, two actors are past fifty, and the rest are professionals in their thirties or early forties with at least a decade of acting experience. They strike me on this first day as an unusually articulate and likeable group of men and women.

Sobel introduces everyone around the improvised table. He takes a moment to explain my presence, which he does with the grace I've already come to expect from him. The actors who are new to the Pearl look at me with a curiosity that is both friendly and fleeting. Actors are not naturally suspicious types—imagine the same scene with a dozen cops!—and people whose job it is to turn their emotions inside out on a stage before strangers are not likely to worry about the presence of another outsider. By the same token, they are too absorbed in their work to concern themselves overly about the observer with the pencil.

The members of the Pearl's resident acting company all know me and what I'm doing. Sobel told me during our first discussion that my project would require their approval, and he arranged an evening meeting at a member's apartment. It was a small fourth-floor walkup in the West Fifties. Sobel and the seven actors, all casually dressed, were sprawled here and there on the floor or the few chairs; a bowl of fruit and crackers stood on the coffee table. The atmosphere of the group was easy and cheerful.

Joanne Camp introduced me with skillful diplomacy. She told the others that in reading something of mine, she'd been impressed with how I let the people I was writing about speak directly to the reader. The message evidently was not lost on the other actors, for they approved my undertaking after a few rather desultory questions. They even began to joke about me. "I say the ladies' dressing room should be off limits unless he learns how to lace up our corsets," an actress declared.

In the next weeks I went to lunch with each of the seven actors in turn. We got on well. I liked what I found: people engaged in a difficult and unusual profession who are both serious and easy to talk with. I saw no swollen egos, and none displayed the exhibitionism we tend to associate with actors. When I asked why they'd become actors, several gave answers suggesting that living the lives of others filled some sort of void they felt in themselves. A tall, gaunt man in his late thirties said: "There's not enough of me. Some of the characters I play are more three-dimensional than I am." A beautiful and seemingly self-confident actress surprised me by saying: "I didn't like myself." But she quickly added: "I've gotten over that!" The youngest member came from a theatre family. "I'm a fairly shy person," she said. "I'd be a mess if I had to come out on stage and say: 'Hi, I'm Laura Rathgeb.' I'm nervous all the time as myself. But when I come out as someone else it's completely different." An actress whose profile suggests tragedy spoke mystically about some of the people whose fictional lives she'd inhabited. She'd so identified with Shaw's Major Barbara, she told me, that she'd cast off a job and a man because that's what Barbara would have done. By contrast, another actress said in response to an overly solemn question: "*Play* is what theatre's about, David. It ain't brain surgery!" And she went off into a raucous laugh.

Much as they differed as individuals, the Pearl actors all spoke easily and with insight about themselves and their lives. It was refreshing to find that none of them reminded me in the least of those other members of their generation who'd chosen the road of greed and were grubbing for other people's money in the brokers' and lawyers' offices two miles south of the Pearl. This was also what I'd come for. We journalists spend too many of our days in enemy territory. If we write about those who make the news, we are with rare exceptions writing about people we dislike and distrust: politicians and tycoons, the manipulators of men and money. (At least we *should* dislike them. A journalist who doesn't do so belongs in public relations.) I wanted to be among people I could respect and enjoy. I was looking forward to spending a season in the company of the Pearl people.

Now the stage manager takes over. David Waggett is a stocky, bearded man of around forty with a decisive, don't-tread-on-my-prerogatives manner. The stage manager is the enforcer of the rules, and Waggett soon lets us know he's well aware of that role. His first action is to send the non-Equity people off the stage for a members-only discussion with the field representative of the Actors' Equity Association, the union that sets the rules under which stage actors work. She's a heavyset woman with an un-smiling mien that sets her apart from everyone else here: where others are cheerily serious, she's solemn, even bureaucratic. Sobel and I leave, and so does young Hank Wagner, the Pearl's apprentice actor. When we are summoned back, after half an hour, Waggett shows the cast a model of the set. It's made of cardboard and is in a box about two feet long and a foot wide. Where are the exits? is the question that most concerns the actors.

The stage manager next spends ten minutes on housekeeping. He calls our attention to his toolbox, in which he has materials for "almost any emergency"—bandages, electrician's tape, small tools, pencils, needle and thread. Does anyone wear contact lenses that risk being stepped on? Any special diets? (This has to do with meals the Pearl will provide for the cast.) Any smokers? No hands go up, though we learn later that fully half of us are ex-smokers, and someone says "Wow!" as if in wonder at the speed of cultural change. (It turns out that one actress does smoke, but not in the theatre.) Waggett says emphatically: "If you don't like the temperature, see me—don't try to change the thermostat yourself." It's hot outside but cold in the theatre. Joanne Camp, who is in her stocking feet, complains of the cold: "My feet are about to fall off." I notice that she is kidding around with the other actors, being very much one of the boys, though she is in fact the Pearl's artistic associate as well as married to the boss.

After a five-minute break—Equity requires five minutes an hour or ten minutes in every ninety minutes—Sobel starts to talk to the actors. He is informal and humorous in his delivery, and it is soon clear he knows exactly what he wants to get across. He begins by talking about the Pearl's move up in status, and draws a laugh when he says: "We're the only theatre in New York— maybe the world!—that's chosen this of all years to expand." (The Pearl is moving this year from Off Off Broadway to Off Broadway without changing its location. Broadway, Off Broadway, and Off Off Broadway are Equity categories that govern the actors' pay and working rules. The designations are no longer defined by geography. The Pearl is moving to a different contract with its actors, not to a different address.)

The change in the Pearl's status is significant both to newcomers and to the theatre's resident actors. A little more money, though still far too little. They'll get $180 a week for eleven weeks: four weeks of rehearsal, seven weeks of performance. All get the same pay whatever their roles. Of that $180 they will actually take home after deductions from $135 to $160. ($180 is about one-third of a Manhattan doorman's starting pay. What's more, his job has an open run and he doesn't have to audition for it.) The actors will get benefits, including unemployment and health insurance, that they didn't get last year; and, less tangibly, they'll find a new importance, a new seriousness, in their work. Acting Off Off Broadway, the Pearl's category in its first seven seasons, is an avocation, it is feeding your habit in the time you can spare from the necessary business of earning a living; such theatres have to arrange rehearsals around the actors' schedules in their other, "straight" jobs. Performing Off Broadway, where we are today, is an actor's primary job. Hardly any of them can live in New York on this pay, so they will still have to work at half a dozen other trades, from typing to teaching. But here—now—acting comes first. Sobel is reminding the actors of those new realities without spelling out the message.

Though the Pearl's new status is clearly good for the actors, it is not without cost to the resident company. In the past the Pearl's actors could count on getting most or all of the choice parts; Sobel would tailor the plays he chose to their abilities or their needs for growth. But now they will have to compete with talented outsiders who previously would not have wanted to work on the Pearl's terms. Already, in fact, Pearl veterans have been passed over for two of the best parts in the play now going into rehearsal.

Sobel turns to Molière's *Tartuffe*, the play that will occupy our attention for the next eleven weeks. (He will direct this first play and one of the other four shows of the season.) No one is coming unprepared. Last spring Sobel told the company his selections for the season, and the outside actors knew from their auditions that they would be playing *Tartuffe*. Sobel tells us that Orgon, the protagonist, is a good man whose mid-life problems have caused him to become obsessed with the religious con man Tartuffe: that's the nub of the story. Orgon takes Tartuffe into his home, where the fraudulent ascetic dictates piety to the household. In his obsession Orgon promises both his unwilling daughter and all his worldly goods to the con man. During the course of the play the members of his family try to warn him of Tartuffe's villainy, but Orgon turns a deaf ear until his wife forces him to watch in hiding as the con man propositions her. By then it seems to be too late, but King Louis XIV intervenes to save a chastened Orgon and his family from ruin. Like all of Molière, *Tartuffe* is a comedy. But the story is also a dark commentary on human nature, and Molière's depiction of religious hypocrisy drew enough blood that the play in its original version was banned for five years.

Sobel tells us that the "solicited audience response," a term he often uses to mean "how we hope the audience will react," is to see on stage exaggerated versions of people we know. Molière is about a balance of extremes, and broad slapstick coexists with subtle irony. "My charge to you is to be very extreme and very controlled." (Asked later for an example, he cites the finely calculated slapstick of Harpo Marx.)

Sobel talks about the thorny matter of Molière's rhymed couplets: not an easy kind of dialogue for American actors. (It is characteristic of Sobel that he chose *Tartuffe* in part for its difficulty, so he and the company could gain experience with a play in couplets.) "These are the cleverest people you'll ever meet," he tells the actors. "They even talk in rhyme. It's not a burden—they delight in it." A minute later he says: "I want to play a seventeenth-century family game. We must talk in rhyme, and finish each other's rhymes." The actors start improvising their own couplets:

Orgon: "Elmire, have you done the wash today?"

Elmire (his wife, played by Joanne Camp): "Orgon, what a terrible thing to say!"

Tartuffe: "I'd like to protest."

Dorine (the maid): "And I'd like to hear the rest!" Julia Glander, the lively blonde playing the maid, claps her hands in glee.

That evening, Sobel will say how pleased he is that the actors were willing to "play my silly game"—a game obviously intended only to help put the cast at ease with the idea of rhymed couplets. He thinks they're off to a good start. He particularly likes the quality of the "jobbers," as outside actors are called: their presence will make the Pearl company "play at the top of their game."

At 12:25 Sobel calls on Joanne Camp to lead the first of what will be daily vocal exercises. It is Sobel's belief that actors need daily vocal and movement exercise as much as musicians need their daily scales. But many actors don't heed that principle, and so, he says, with the hyperbole he often uses to underline a point, "If I won the lottery tomorrow, I'd close the Pearl for eight months of training. Then I'd put on a season." The Pearl's exercises were designed by Robert Neff Williams, a voice and diction teacher at Juilliard who has led workshops for the past three seasons at the Pearl. The actors now make a circle, and, after a few getting-ready movements—bouncing around to loosen the shoulder and neck—Camp leads them in exercises designed to increase their vocal range and sharpen their enunciation. She takes them from the bottom to the top of their range with an ironically apt rhyme that we'll hear endlessly repeated: up from the bottom with "Lured by the strumpet Fame's fair charms," then back down again from "charms" at the top with "He died in the hag Oblivion's arms." Today they're finding the natural range of their voices; in later days they will try to increase that range, stretching their voices ever higher on "charms" without going falsetto. (Camp says one of her great problems as a young actress was a voice that got shrill and unpleasant in the upper register; the voice she had to use when she was most expressive was hard on the ears of the audience. She attributes her retraining of that voice to the workshops with Williams.) The exercises Camp is leading will increase the contrast they can give to their lines. An actor varies the pitch of his voice to call attention to a transition of some sort; in the case of Molière's couplets, a change of pitch also serves to avoid singsong rhymes. Next Camp starts exercises designed to sharpen the actors' enunciation: "What a to-do to die today at a minute or two to two." We Americans are naturally sloppy in our diction, so our actors have far to go for clarity of speech. Clear enunciation is of course particularly important to acting on stage. When performing for film or television, actors can afford to slur because the microphone will come in close to pick up their words. But on even a small stage like the Pearl's the actors have to project forty feet to people in the last row without electronic assistance. (Most larger theatres, however, now use microphones.) For this play, clarity of speech is indispensable: a story that takes place in seventeenth-century Paris and is told in translated rhymed couplets is bound at times to be hard to follow, impossible if you miss too many of the words.

The stage manager announces a ten-minute break, and when we come back it is 1:10 and time for the first reading of *Tartuffe*. During the break, we've moved the two scarred tables over to the wall; behind them sit the stage manager and his young woman apprentice, and me. The actors are sitting scattered around the stage. They are holding production copies, with the text enlarged; they've highlighted their own lines with Magic Marker. Sobel, standing, says to them: "This is our first reading. We don't know how the story will end, so this is your first and best chance to affect the outcome." Sobel is referring to two important ideas. One is the "first time": that to keep the audience's attention the actors must persuade us that they do not know what is going to happen any more than we do—that this is the first time for them also. The other is that the actor's preeminent task on stage is to try to affect his scene partner, the person on stage with him, to try to persuade the other to do or believe what the actor's character wants (rather than to express emotion or to aim lines eloquently at the audience). "Move around during the reading if you want. I won't interrupt: it's all yours."

The actors read with surprising fluency, although they have not memorized their lines and are speaking many if not all of those lines for what is indeed the first time. Years ago, appearing at first rehearsal with lines memorized would have been a point in an actor's favor, but today many theatre people believe that learning the lines before their meaning has been explored in rehearsal can lead to mechanical acting. Joanne Camp, sitting cross-legged on the stage floor, reddish-blond hair flowing around her shoulders, gives her lines much of the time without the book, but that is because she's had to learn many of those lines when she served as scene partner to the actors auditioning for the parts of Tartuffe and Dorine.

Martin LaPlatney was chosen by Sobel to play the villain of the piece. He is a big, powerfully built man in his early forties, not at all the physical type I imagined for the reptilian Tartuffe. Camp, who has performed with him before, describes him as "a marvelous, outrageous actor." (That more than one hundred actors, all experienced professionals, applied for a part paying $180 a week tells us how desperate actors are for opportunities to practice their trade. Candidates came from Toronto and Boston to audition for Dorine. Of the applicants for Tartuffe, Sobel auditioned thirty.)

Watching auditions—in this case a dozen would-be Tartuffes playing the same scene—is an emphatic reminder of how much the players bring to the play. Six weeks earlier I'd sat alongside Sobel watching a series of actors trying out for Tartuffe as they played that scene, an attempted seduction, with Joanne Camp. Sobel sat in a middle-row seat behind a big homemade desk designed to fit over the seat in front of him. On the desk was a pile of the actors' photos and professional biographies sent to the Pearl by their agents. Each audition lasted about ten minutes. Sobel sat very still during the auditions. Some actors he simply thanked, and others he asked to redo part of the scene with a different approach. "Try it as a salesman closing a deal," he said to a small, scrawny black actor with a West Indian accent. Once, however, he stopped the actor, a tall, quiet young man, in the middle of the scene and said gently: "You're doing a good job, but it's the wrong part for you. We'll call you for others." Between two auditions Camp yawned, sat down briefly, and told me she hadn't slept the night before; but, a real trouper, she was always fresh for still another playing of that same scene. The actors I saw audition represented a wide variety of physical types. A cadaverous youth was followed by an obese actor of about the same age. Only a sharp-featured olive-skinned man, who stood bent forward at the waist, had the sinister appearance I expected. One athletic young man asked about the attempted seduction: "Is it romantic? Or is he an anal-retentive desperate for it?" The actors had prepared the scene at home and they played it in very different ways. Of one candidate my notes read in part: "Tall, blond. Much more gesture, movement. Overdone, farce. Prostrates self at slave line, pretends bite JC [Camp]. JC laughs at end, pushes him. SS [Sobel]: Redo speech, be confident of conquest. JC: Only audition where I almost had my crotch bitten."

That, I learned much later, was the actor now playing Tartuffe; he was chosen after a second audition, known as a "callback." Many of the interpretations I saw that day were plausible, at least to me; any of these men and any of these readings could be Tartuffe. These dozen versions of Tartuffe—and many more, past and future—all found their source in the words that Molière wrote. Nor will we ever know the person the author saw in his mind's eye as he wrote his lines; Molière, unlike Shaw, left us no explanations of his characters. So, I realized, actors can paint any number of portraits from the same sketch drawn by Molière's lines, each of them claiming with equal legitimacy to be Tartuffe.

Our Tartuffe is playing his part to the hilt already. Martin LaPlatney is making himself noticed. The other actors stay more or less put while they read, but not LaPlatney. During his seduction scene with Joanne Camp, he takes off his shirt, displaying his muscular physique, and climbs across a chair to get at her. I wonder if he is in any way testing the man who is his director and her husband. Later Sobel observes mildly that "Martin is playing the class clown."

We finish the reading at 2:55. Sobel, who has been sitting to one side taking notes, says: "It's a great cast and a great play. If it's messed up, it'll be by me." We break for lunch. No one can afford a restaurant, though one actor goes out for a pizza. Most of the actors have brought food from home in brown paper bags on which they carefully write their names before putting them in the Pearl's refrigerator. By the fridge, the sign on a coffee machine says: I'M CHEAP BUT I'M NOT FREE. 25 CENTS PLEASE. A few heat their food in the microwave, which the actors consider to be one of the Pearl's notable amenities. They settle to eat in twos and threes in the two dressing rooms, on stage, and especially, on this August day, in the little backyard, a greater amenity that will serve us well throughout the four weeks of rehearsal. Here the three creaky metal chairs are quickly preempted, a couple of actors have to stand to eat, and our one smoker can satisfy her habit.

At 4:05 we're back on the stage and Sobel is introducing Richard Morse, a Molière specialist whom he earlier described to us as "a nut, a really brilliant nut." He is here to teach the actors the highly stylized movement of the seventeenth century. The person who appears on the stage is a paunchy man in late middle age, with wild graying hair, dressed in baggy sweatpants and a ragged sweatshirt. He's wearing ballet shoes and carrying a tambourine. He starts a tape of period music. "It's like dance class—take the first position," he says, and soon he has the actors moving in ways that are unfamiliar to most and to some very difficult. No movement of that time comes naturally to twentieth-century Americans; just walking across a Molière room is a finely calculated exercise that had to be precisely executed if you were to be socially acceptable. It's hard on both the actors' legs and on their attention. I notice, however, that all the actors, whatever their age, are in excellent physical condition: it's a profession that makes heavy demands on your body and your stamina. As I look over those present, I reflect unhappily that fewer excess pounds are to be seen on the eleven actors on the stage than on the four of us watching them from the audience.

In Molière's day, the style Morse is teaching was not something laid on top of one's personality; it expressed one's identity in the world. Louis XIV had codified the rules of style in an apparent effort to make the members of the upper classes display in their very movements the values considered proper to them. These values were, Morse tells us, to display (at least to one's peers) generosity, courage, and openness—the arms are always open to the other people in the room. All movements should be musical, graceful, light. Morse shows us what he means with his own person: when this middle-aged man with flab around his waist moves across the stage, he floats as weightless as a ballerina.

The actors respond very differently to what Morse is offering. Stylized movement seems to come more naturally to the women, and Julia Glander, our Dorine, who has the supple body of a dancer, looks completely at home with even the most difficult exercises; she later tells me that she spent a couple of years as a mime. It's much harder for the men, and especially for a couple of big, strongly built actors. Seventeenth-century movement does not seem to suit muscular male bodies, and what is graceful on a woman may in our time look effeminate on a man. Martin LaPlatney, our Tartuffe, barely pretends to do the exercises: he is, once again, setting himself apart from the others.

Richard Morse is a veteran actor who once directed his own mime theatre, where he gave Sobel his first acting job in New York. He now teaches in the Midwest, and is in New York to put on a one-man show at the Pearl titled *Molière*. (Sobel bartered the use of the theatre for the workshops Morse is now teaching.) The night I saw it Morse played to an enthusiastic full house. The story takes place in Molière's last moments; he died backstage after the fourth performance of his *The Imaginary Invalid*, in which he played the title role. As Molière, Morse recounts the great events of the playwright's career. He ends with an anecdote that somehow sums up his subject. When I died (says Morse as Molière) I went to the place where God lives. He wasn't there, so to pass the time I invented some people. I was playing with them—Morse moves his hands as if he were holding marionettes on strings—when God returned. He asked me what I was doing, and when I explained, God said: "Oh. . . . That's what I always wanted to do."

Morse's workshop ends the first day of rehearsal. It's six o'clock. I remind Sobel that he told me he would know "by 11:15" if the rehearsal was going to be a success. Was it? "A qualified yes," Sobel says. Those qualifications had to do with two actors, the newcomer Martin LaPlatney as Tartuffe, and a Pearl veteran, Frank Geraci, as the protagonist Orgon. But that did not become clear to me until weeks later.

〇৬ AUGUST 7

9:30: The Fire Department appears unexpectedly in the persons of five uniformed men at the door. They're all white, and they all speak in working-class accents with the somewhat hostile swagger that goes with their coplike position. They're here for one of their periodic inspections. Sobel calls out for Mary Harpster, the Pearl's general manager, and he takes refuge in the backyard. "I'm the kind who always gets a ticket," he says. "Mary handles it much better." The firemen meanwhile have climbed to the roof and will work their way down to the cellar— they are checking for emergency exits, extinguishers, and flammable materials. They leave after half an hour, and we later learn that the theatre got a clean bill of fire health.

At 11:00, after Joanne Camp has led the daily vocal warm-up, we start work on I.1: the opening scene. The author introduces the theme and sets the tone of the play by presenting half a dozen characters as seen through the comically distorted lens of Madame Pernelle, mother of the protagonist, Orgon. She comes storming on stage, followed by the members of her son's family, whom she proceeds to introduce by denouncing each in turn. In the course of her harangues we learn about the presence in the household of the holy man Tartuffe, whom the mother and son admire and whom the rest of the family think is a fraud. On her way out, frustrated by her inability to control her son's family, she slaps her maid instead.

The actors read through the scene. They are standing on stage holding their scripts. They look at the character they are addressing, but otherwise make no attempt to move about the stage. They are still wearing not Seventeenth-Century Formal but the Late-Twentieth-Century Casual of jeans and shorts. The stage manager, David Waggett, is sitting to the side of the stage, with five of the English translations of the play, a French text, and a French-English dictionary in front of him. Sobel is sitting in a first-row seat. "We need to know what events we're coming from," he says after the reading. "What caused Madame Pernelle to storm out like that?" A play, after all, covers only a brief moment (one day, in the case of *Tartuffe*) in the lives of its characters. That's all the author tells us. In order to understand what happens during that day, and to present it persuasively to the audience, the actors and director must agree on what was happening to these people before the play began. It's an exploration that will continue on and off through the early weeks of rehearsal. The mental scripts they write are their own, not Molière's, part of their contribution to the collaboration between actors and author that makes the show the audience will see.

"You need a clear idea of how you would have liked the afternoon to go—how it would have gone in the time of your son's first wife," Sobel says to the actress playing Madame Pernelle. "I've just heard them all complaining about Tartuffe," says Madame Pernelle. "They wouldn't dare do that if Orgon [her son] weren't away. They won't pay attention to me, not even Elmire [Orgon's much younger second wife]. That's what infuriates me." Elmire's brother observes that he too must have been away, since he hasn't met this Tartuffe everyone's talking about. Joanne Camp, as Elmire, suggests that the members of the family have all been telling her brother about the trouble the religious interloper is causing them. "How long has Tartuffe been living with you?" Sobel asks. Two weeks, says Camp. Another actor guesses two months. To Dorine, the maid, who has two long speeches in the scene, Sobel says: "Try to arrange your thoughts to stress one point in each speech."

At 12:45 Sobel interrupts rehearsal for a brief refresher exercise in the movements taught by Richard Morse. The exercises are led by Julia Glander, our lively Dorine in biking shorts. I imagine Molière sitting beside me and chuckling as he watches the actors in their jeans and shorts moving in the stylized patterns of his seventeenth century. He would have loved the incongruity of it.

By four o'clock we are working on scene 3. Sobel and the three actors in the scene are sitting in a semicircle on stage. Scene 3 introduces the protagonist, Orgon. It is the most difficult moment in the play, and neither Sobel nor Frank Geraci, who plays Orgon, will ever be satisfied with their interpretation of it. Orgon is returning home from his brief absence. The household scatters at his arrival, but he is able to collar the maid. "How has everything gone?" he asks.

> DORINE: Madame had a bad fever, two days ago,
> And a headache that really brought her low.
> ORGON: Yes. And Tartuffe?
> DORINE: Tartuffe? Fit as a fiddle:
> Red mouth, pink cheeks, and bulging at the middle.
> ORGON: Poor fellow!

The exchange is repeated three times. Each time Dorine adds to the details of his wife's illness, and tells him of Tartuffe's gross behavior. At last her mistress is treated with bleeding, the maid says. To Orgon's "Yes. And Tartuffe?" Dorine says: "To make up for the blood Madame had lost/He downed at breakfast four great drafts of wine." And for the fourth time Orgon responds only: "Poor fellow!"

The scene can be played as mere farce, and Orgon as an idiot, but Sobel is asking the difficult question: What is going through Orgon's mind that brings that strange response? Stanislavski, who was rehearsing *Tartuffe* when he died in 1938, once observed that characters say only ten percent of what they are thinking: it is up to the actor to reconstruct the rest. This archeology of the mind is of course unusually difficult when the evidence is as scanty as it is in this scene. Orgon gives us far less than ten percent. Those two words—"Poor fellow!"—are the only clue to his thoughts. That was enough for Molière, but then he not only wrote the play, he played Orgon himself. He knew what his Orgon was thinking; others playing the role have to figure it out.

The snapshot above is a reminder that my first experience of theatre, long before the Pearl, was with Stanislavski himself. Here he is in an impromptu disguise of clothespins and a woman's handbag, clowning for a five-year-old boy—me. With him is the actor Leonid Leonidov. My mother, Elizabeth Reynolds Hapgood, shown at right, translated Stanislavski's works on acting. Note that the bag in her hand is Stanislavski's beard in the other photo.

Shepard Sobel and Joanne Camp are married to each other and to the Pearl. Sobel has directed Camp in several of the many roles she has played at the Pearl, when she wasn't acting on Broadway or at another Off Broadway theatre.

Before almost any performance Sobel can be found, as above, in the Pearl's tiny lobby, "schmoozing" with the audience. The photos on the wall are of scenes from past productions at the Pearl. Below, Sobel watches from a first-row seat during the complex task of dismantling one unit and erecting its successor.

Much of the work involved in
changing shows is done by volunteers who are known as "friends of
the Pearl." Above, one such friend
is adjusting a light over the stage.
Of course, Sobel is always there,
climbing a ladder or hauling a
piece of the set.

Stanislavski asked his Orgon to visualize his thoughts when he hears what Dorine is telling him. He realizes (Stanislavski suggested) that the commotion in the household over his sick wife is interrupting Tartuffe's all-important communication with God—hence the first "Poor fellow!" When Dorine tells him about the wine at breakfast, Orgon recalls that his holy man is not a drinker and concludes that Tartuffe must be greatly upset about his wife's illness, which Tartuffe's prayers no doubt healed, though no one in the household will give him credit for it— "Poor fellow!" Thus Orgon's response makes sense in the context of his obsession with the religious salvation he thinks Tartuffe is bringing him.

Frank Geraci had discussed his preparation for Orgon a month earlier, in mid-July. We were sitting in the small apartment near the Holland Tunnel that he shares with Wooster, a gray cat named for the street where he was found as a kitten. On arriving I'd noticed evidence that Geraci, like most actors, is concerned with keeping himself fit. There's a bicycle he takes out on day-long rides to Coney Island or the outer edges of Queens, and in the kitchen area I see a juicer in which he squeezes out healthful concoctions. He's also a reader: the walls are lined with bookshelves.

Geraci is a small, slender man of fifty-one, with closely cropped graying hair, and an on-and-off beard that's gray when it's on, as it then was. He was cordial, open to my interrogation, and he talked easily about his profession. There was about him an indefinable air of loneliness and perhaps sadness for which at the time I could find no explanation. Geraci had invited me for lunch, which turned out to be a dietarily correct but tasteful potage of chicken and potatoes. It was, we noted, a dish that Orgon might have eaten in his Paris home.

Orgon was very much with us that day. Geraci had begun preparing for the role. He was reading up on the period, looking at pictures to get its visual feel, and as we talked, music of Molière's time was playing in the background. Most of all,

Geraci had begun to seek his version of Orgon. He was looking for the unconscious wellsprings of Orgon's behavior. "The closer you get to your character's unconscious desires," he said, "the more energy you have." The question concerning the play's protagonist is this: why cannot Orgon, an otherwise intelligent and mature man, see what everyone else in the household, beginning with Dorine in the "Poor fellow!" scene, is trying to point out to him—that Tartuffe is a fraud who is exploiting him? Geraci believed that Orgon is willfully blind, that "at some deep level he knows that Tartuffe is a crook and a hypocrite," though on another level he sees him as offering spiritual salvation. (At this early stage of his preparation, Geraci was developing theories to account for his character's behavior that he knew he might later discard in favor of other explanations: they would serve their purpose if they helped him get into Orgon's skin.)

In Geraci's view, Orgon is engaged in a guerrilla war with his mother, the formidable Madame Pernelle, whom we saw in action in the opening scene. He's using Tartuffe as a weapon in this war. His mother wants to dictate piety in the household because she doesn't like his attractive new wife? He'll find another preacher of piety to do it instead, so that she cannot lay down the law to him—so there, Maman! In his search for the parental origins of Orgon's present behavior, Geraci inevitably reaches into his past to draw on the emotions that accompanied his troubled relations with his own mother. (This is what Stanislavski called "emotion memory." The actor seeks in the events of his life the emotions he needs for his character.)

Before rehearsal, Geraci said, he would work on Orgon's outward self—his way of moving. "This will get me out of my body movements and into his." He would, for example, get accustomed to the stick that Orgon carried. In many scenes Orgon makes a point of not listening to what the others are telling him; Geraci intended to work out possible movements for these scenes himself. He does this, he said, for fear of being "put in a straitjacket by the director, especially this director, because of his limited imagination." This was my first suggestion that

Geraci did not anticipate a smooth journey with Sobel directing his Orgon.

He would also work out a "physical line" that would give purpose to Orgon's entrances and exits. "It's essential that I know where I came from, why I'm on stage, and where I'm going when I leave." Geraci would draw a line from point *A*, where he was, through the stage, to point *B*, where he's going. In the case of his first scene, Orgon may have bought a "huge present" for Tartuffe on his trip and, when on stage, be on his way to take it to his religious guide. So the people he encounters are obstacles in his path to Tartuffe, the source of his spiritual salvation, and his purpose in the scene is to get rid of those obstacles. "So when I leave I'm not exiting the stage, I'm going someplace. You can even hear the difference in an actor's voice, whether it drops off or stays up when he's exiting."

Geraci had been mulling over Orgon's relations with the other characters. When he saw Joanne Camp, with whom he was taking a workshop in speech, he thought about her as his stage wife, Elmire. He asked himself why he'd married her, and how she differed from his first wife. (Actually these two Pearl veterans have been stage spouses more often than either can easily recall.) The maid, Dorine, he was sure, had more street smarts than he (either Orgon or Geraci), and that would infuse his relations with her with a touch of envy and fear. "People think because I'm from Brooklyn I must have street smarts, but I don't." Geraci noted that the actors playing Tartuffe and Orgon's brother-in-law, Cléante, were both over six feet tall, compared to his own five feet five. Camp's Elmire was also taller than Geraci's Orgon, so, he said, "there'll be a thing about the talls and the shorts."

After lunch our conversation turned to the actor's life. Geraci has spent most of the last eight years working at the Pearl. He stays there, despite low pay and frequent disagreement with Sobel's directing, because of the roles he can play. "I'm always working on good scripts when I'm doing classics," he said. "The playwright is saying something way down deep, so it's worth the search to find it. I can always find purpose in a good character."

Orgon is not his first Molière at the Pearl. Two years ago he played the lead in *The Imaginary Invalid.* "That was a wonderful vaudeville romp," he recalled. "I hope we can keep it that way, but maybe we were braver then." The atmosphere at the Pearl helps this highly self-critical actor combat the laziness of which he suspects himself. "The time at the Pearl has shown me the value of patience. There are enough people around giving the message that if you're willing to keep on working, we can make it better. If you don't want to keep working, you can rely on tricks, and a new audience each night will like you anyway." He wondered if wanting to be liked by the audience had spoiled his performance a year earlier as the villain, Angelo, in Shakespeare's *Measure for Measure.* He hadn't made the "animal lunge" the role required. "Was it this puerile thing, the need to hear the audience say 'You were wonderful'? I hope not, but every actor has that need."

The speech workshop he was attending was a return to basics: the diction that is essential to stage speech. "It feels like coming in new again, after all these years," he said, a note of weariness in his voice. "But I don't mind, I really don't mind." He recalled with pleasure doing Molière couplets with Joanne Camp in the workshop. "It's fun doing couplets when you finish your partner's rhyme, or she finishes yours. You know you and your partner have to be together verbally and physically, like acrobats on a trapeze."

"It's tough work, acting, it really is," he said later, his voice rising. "There's a point in any role where you don't know where the hell you are, and you wonder, will I ever learn this. I don't find it gets any easier the older I get. At fifty-one, some part of me is looking forward to some kind of retirement. Another part of me says you're never going to retire. No matter how long you work, you're going to have to keep on working to make it better."

That second evening of rehearsal, after the players have left, Sobel is also musing about the actor's life. We are sitting in the Pearl's backyard. Around us are the backs of old-style New York apartment houses; at this hot time of year we see a few deck chairs on their fire escapes. The late-summer sun touches the old buildings with welcome dabs of gold. Sobel is relaxing after rehearsal, but only for a few minutes. He has hours of work ahead of him—the clerical and maintenance work that keeps the operation going—before he can go home. We've been talking about what an actor needs to play Molière. I am impressed by how the actors rise to the intellectual demands of their roles. This, I observe, contradicts the stereotype of the actor as child-like, almost an idiot savant: someone who is emotionally gifted but otherwise not very smart and who therefore needs to be told by the director what his character is thinking. "There are no dumb actors, not when you're doing a classic, and Molière is especially hard," Sobel says. "We're asking so very much of them. They have to do forty-eight things at once." He shakes his head. "It's a tough job," he says, echoing Frank Geraci.

⟍⟍ AUGUST 8

11:00: Of the five people on stage, two are actors. It occurs to me that the others are ground crew who make it possible for the actors to take off into a world we will never know. Only the actors will experience the thrill of flight. Only the actors will explore their own multiple identities in their search for the common humanity that links them to the characters they inhabit. Only the actors have the power to sway the emotions of the audience. The rest of us are bound to this earth and to our own selves. Is it to balance that thrill of flight on some cosmic scale that the actor's life is otherwise so very hard?

We're working on act II, scene 3. The scene is between Dorine, the maid, and Mariane, daughter of Orgon. They've just learned that Orgon, in his obsession with the religious con man

Tartuffe, has decided to make his daughter give up her sweet-heart and marry Tartuffe. The comic force of the scene lies in the contrast between the maid, who will do anything to thwart her master's plan, and the daughter, who is afraid to do anything at all.

The two actresses, both in shorts, are sitting at a small table on stage. They're discussing the scene with Sobel, who sits at a nearby table. Dorine is played by Julia Glander, the blond one-time mime, and Mariane by Kathryn Lee.

Kathryn Lee was born in Korea thirty-one years ago. "I was abandoned by my Korean parents," she said in a quiet tone. "My American parents think I was born in a village and left in Seoul in a place where they knew I'd be taken to an orphanage. Apparently it wasn't all that uncommon at the time." She was in fact taken to an orphanage and adopted by an American couple who brought her to this country when she was seven months old. In answer to my question she said: "I feel some curiosity about my Korean parents, but less than I did when I was younger. I don't think I'd have a chance in a thousand of finding them. Even if I did, I'd find it very difficult to communicate with them. I don't speak any Korean." After a moment she adds: "America is the only culture I know."

Lee's presence reflects the Pearl's commitment to race-blind casting. The subject was much discussed in the New York theatre community that fall, because of the controversy over casting the musical *Miss Saigon* (for which Lee auditioned). I asked her what kind of roles she'd been playing. Mostly Asian and what she called "nonspecific" roles, though when she played Juliet she was the only Asian in that cast.

Tartuffe is the first play in which she is playing a member of what is so unmistakably a European family; what's more, her father and brother are on stage at the same time she is. Lee arrived at the Pearl wondering whether anyone would think the ethnic disparity needed explaining to the audience. "I didn't trust them enough. I was very pleased to find out they didn't need to do that," she said. By the third day, in fact, Lee and the others are joking about their own explanation: Orgon's house was served by an Asian iceman.

Sobel and the actors are exploring Mariane, the character Lee is playing. They speculate about her upbringing and her habits: what kind of books does she read? Romance novels. "Her reality is a romantic reality," Sobel says. "When she says her only choices are suicide or a nunnery if her father won't let her marry the man she loves—she really believes it. Dorine knows there are less drastic choices, and so does the audience, but not Mariane."

To Julia Glander, Sobel observes that the maid, Dorine, seems descended from Columbine, the commedia dell'arte figure that Glander played years earlier. Both are servants who manipulate their masters. Dorine is the only character who shows herself to be aware of the audience. Often when she could end a scene she keeps it going simply because she and the audience are enjoying what's happening. "Work your logic," he says when she is unsure about Dorine's motives, and in a few minutes Glander bursts out: "I see it! I see the logic!"

After two readings and a break, we move on to the following scene. This introduces Valère, the young man Mariane loves. He comes on stage having learned that his sweetheart's father has promised her to Tartuffe. There follows a lovers' quarrel in which each waits for the other to break the social code that regulates their behavior. Neither does, and Valère storms dramatically off. Dorine—once again the force driving the action—summons him back and manipulates the two lovers into a reconciliation.

For the second reading, Sobel asks the actors to change places so that Glander is in the middle. While the lovers are quarreling, her Dorine looks back and forth between them with eyebrows raised and eyes wide open. She steals the scene with such comic skill that all of us, actors and ground crew alike, are laughing too hard to continue. "They do the work and you get the laughs," Sobel says to Glander.

During the lunch break I find Sobel and David Waggett, the stage manager, in the corridor that leads from the stage past the dressing rooms to the yard. Waggett holds a copy of *Back Stage* from which he is reading aloud a list of theatres that have received grants from the National Endowment for the Arts. He asks how much the Pearl got, and Sobel makes a zero sign with thumb and forefinger. The two observe that the theatres that get the most funding seem to be those with the biggest administrative overhead, which means the highest offstage salaries. "More of our budget goes to actors than at any other theatre in New York," Sobel observes. He says this in his usual low-keyed way, but I know by now that this is a point of great pride with him.

4:15: After the daily movement exercises, led by Julia Glander, Sobel reminds the actors of the importance of diction and pronunciation: "You've got some homework to do—we have to standardize our speech. 'Interest' has three syllables. It's 'that you,' not 'tha chew.' " To Dorine he says: "When you say 'goodbye' let me hear the *d*. Otherwise it's twentieth century."

4:45: Martin LaPlatney and Joanne Camp are reading the scene in which his Tartuffe first propositions Camp as Orgon's wife, Elmire, while Sobel—Elmire's offstage husband—watches from the third row. Once again LaPlatney seems to be wildly overplaying the scene. Although they are still sitting and reading from their scripts, LaPlatney climbs onto Camp's chair and tries to fondle her. She seems amused by his antics. To Sobel he says: "I'm trying anything that comes into my head. You tell me what works." Sobel doesn't respond.

6:15: The actors have gone and the crew is coming in to set up the stage for the evening performance of Richard Morse's Molière show. Sobel and I are in the orchestra. It's a broiling August day, as hot in the theatre as it is outside, and one young man rather anxiously asks Sobel: "Is it all right if I take my shirt off?" "Sure," Sobel says, and then, amused at the idea that his permission is needed, he adds, straight-faced: "As a matter of fact, we've had a couple of requests." I chuckle, but the line falls flat with its intended audience: the young man stares blankly. Sobel shrugs and murmurs: "Oh well."

AUGUST 9

This morning's rehearsal centers on Cléante, brother to Orgon's wife, Elmire. Cléante is the voice of reason in the story.

"Cléante is a man of the Renaissance, a believer in the power of reason," Sobel says to Dugg Smith, the actor playing Cléante. "He's confident that people will listen to his advice. No one ever does listen, but he never loses his confidence that they will. That's the comedy in his scenes with Orgon and Tartuffe."

We start with Cléante's first scene with his brother-in-law. He's just witnessed Orgon's strange behavior in the "Poor fellow!" scene. When they're alone he asks for an explanation. Orgon launches into a wild tirade about how Tartuffe has remade his life:

> He guides me on new paths in new directions,
> Trains me to mortify all my affections,
> And liberates my soul from every tie.

Cléante now has a long speech in which he denounces religious hypocrisy and praises people of reason and freedom of thought. This may well be a softened version of the lines that caused *Tartuffe* to be banned. Louis XIV banned the play at the insistence of the religious authorities of Paris, though he was a patron of Molière's and had himself enjoyed *Tartuffe.* Molière rewrote the script twice before he succeeded in getting the King to lift the ban. Only the third of the three versions survives, so we will never know what Molière really wanted to say about religion. Still, the message in the approved text is clear enough so that *Tartuffe* has remained a symbol prized by French free-thinkers ever since. Whenever reaction and religious sanctimony prevail, as in the Bourbon Restoration of the 1820s and the Vichy government of the Second World War, *Tartuffe* is staged as a form of protest.

Cléante's speech runs eighty-three lines, with a single brief interruption. It's extremely difficult to deliver that many lines of rhymed couplets without lapsing into singsong and losing the audience. "Start low, you've got a long way to go," Sobel suggests. Throughout the weeks of rehearsal he and Dugg Smith will search for ways to make the long speech move, in order to, in Sobel's words, "keep the audience leaning forward in their seats."

Smith and Frank Geraci, as Orgon, read the scene four or five times. They're still using their scripts, but they're on their feet and have begun trying out ways to move around the stage. Geraci—who appears today in knee-length shorts and a pirate's bandana, a kind of Short John Silver—is having his own troubles with the logic of the scene. What can he be doing during Cléante's speech, and why?

Cléante's next scene is a confrontation with the villain, Tartuffe. (The scene comes much later in the play. Scenes are often rehearsed out of sequence in consideration for the actors. Bunching an actor's scenes together today will give him a day off tomorrow.) "How perceptive is Cléante?" Sobel asks. They agree that Cléante, who thinks somehow that good sense must prevail, cannot fully understand the villainy of Tartuffe. It's an advantage that all con men enjoy when they are dealing with the rest of us: the Cléantes of this world cannot quite bring themselves to believe that the Tartuffes are as evil, as impervious to the voice of reason, as they really are.

I find Dugg Smith in the Pearl's backyard during the lunch break. He's a big, brown-haired man with rather craggy features. He's about Shep Sobel's age, and his relaxed manner and understated masculinity remind me a bit of Sobel: they are both easy men to like. Smith is not a newcomer here. He's worked at the Pearl off and on since its earliest days.

We talk about the crisis that afflicts many male actors in mid-career. "It comes in your late thirties and early forties," Smith says. "It's when you realize you'll never be a star, never get rich acting, always live in insecurity. And you're still young enough to learn another trade. When you're older it's too late to change careers; when you're younger you still have the hope of hitting the jackpot. But at that age we talk about it all the time. Should we give up acting?"

Smith himself did quit, in the fall of 1986, when he was thirty-eight and recently divorced. "I was exasperated by my inability to make a living by acting," he says. During two years out of the theatre he worked as a bartender, then as assistant manager of a diet center in Brooklyn. The money was good, but the work was unpleasant and it promised no better a future. His way back to acting led through the Theatre Development Fund, a nonprofit organization that promotes attendance at live theatre. A member of the Pearl company got him a job there which he still has. TDF allows him to take unpaid leaves in order to act, and all Smith's vacation time has also gone to performance. He's taking out insurance against the future. He'll find time to work at TDF during the run of *Tartuffe*. He's setting aside his pay from the Pearl to buy a Macintosh, on which he intends to learn computer graphics. This, he hopes, will provide him with a second trade he can fall back on when he needs it.

Insecurity afflicts actors at almost all levels of the profession. Dugg Smith recalls the actor who applied for a job at TDF while he was earning excellent pay in a Broadway show. "This show will close, and I'm tired of shows closing, of the uncertainty about when I'm going to work again," the actor explained. "I've got a wife and a child and I can't go on living this way."

Sobel believes career pressure is greatest on "straight male actors over thirty." To be accepted in American society, a male of that age must be earning at least a secure living. (Gay actors, on the other hand, already know "they're never going to get the *Good Housekeeping* seal of approval.") The resulting shortage means that it's hard for Sobel to find "strong male leads" in roles that call for a man in his fifties: "By that time in their lives they're either out of the business or unwilling to work for what the Pearl can pay." Once in a while, though, a successful film actor who started on the stage wants to come back for a show, and sometimes, according to Sobel, male actors will come to the Pearl just to work with Joanne Camp.

Sobel is saying: "I have some hope this ruse has worked, that other people will think I was a fellow dedicated to his causes, artistic, political, and social, and that that's why I did the things I did. But I don't really believe that." He has agreed to talk about his life before the Pearl. We're sitting at a round glass table in the two-room apartment he shares with his wife, Joanne Camp. Behind Sobel is a big bookcase whose shelves are devoted entirely to plays. We're sipping red wine and nibbling blue cheese that is, he says, "all I could find in the refrigerator."

Shepard Sobel is a child of the 1960s, the decade of his adolescence and his early twenties. Born in Manhattan in 1947, he spent his high school years on the south shore of Long Island. His father started an insurance business, which he ultimately had to sell because none of his three sons wanted to follow in his footsteps. "I enormously admired my dad," Sobel recalls. "Achievement was important to me, as it is in many Jewish families, and I always wanted to make proud the parents." He first sought to achieve in athletics. He followed his older brother into the garage and watched him lift weights; he tried out for wrestling and for tennis. In college—Hobart, in upstate New York—he tasted several fields without finding his vocation. "I majored in philosophy, I majored in religion, I majored in everything," he says. Theatre was already a hobby—he acted in school and college plays, and at a community theatre on Long Island during his summers—but in those years he didn't think of it as a career.

"Just look at the pattern," Sobel replies when I ask about the "ruse" he claims to be perpetrating: "Civil rights activist before it was generally accepted, protesting Vietnam before it was mainstream, and now the theatre. It was an era of alternative choices, and I think I opted for fields that were admirable to choose so I could be an achiever. That was often not to my credit but to my benefit. It all looks to me as if that young man was thinking, God, I can't be a county champion at wrestling, my tennis swing doesn't get any better, but theatre—and political and social activism—present a bit of glory, and you got that glory just by doing it, you didn't have to be a county champion at it. That's a problem with American theatre. When you call your mother and say you moved to New York and 'Gee, Mom, it's such a tough profession,' and she says, 'Gosh, I know, you've chosen such a hard row to hoe, just staying with it is a mark of some courage.' That had an appeal for a kid who was reasonably athletic but no champ, who was reasonably bright but no straight-A student, who had no trouble being fairly personable and considerate, no trouble with putting in long hours, and who had no trouble with having a lot of people frowning on his activities, because that was a vote of confidence in its own right. It was rather glorious that my fiancée's family strongly objected to my lack of serious ambition, because I was ruining any career I might have in law [Sobel applied to law school but never went] by being a political activist, or not taking money-making seriously because I was trying to be an actor."

He didn't try to be an actor until several years after college. His first job was teaching English and running the theatre program at Canandaigua High School in the Finger Lakes region of upstate New York. One of the students he directed, Robin Leslie Brown, later became a member of the Pearl company. She remembered the consideration Sobel showed her when he was a first-year teacher and she a high school freshman. After playing a "huge role" in *J.B.*, Brown auditioned for *The Miracle Worker* and was cast in a part with just one line. "I was crushed," Brown told me. "But Shep called me at home that night and said, 'I want you to know your audition was great and I loved everything you did. In a school environment we have to pass the roles around so everybody can experience the joy of acting. I want you to take on this role and do it with as much zeal as you did your part in *J.B.*' It was a good lesson in company performing, and it was what I experienced here at the Pearl, where my first part was a big one, and was immediately followed by much smaller roles. Besides, if you play only leads, you never know what it is to make the play happen, because the lead never does that."

Sobel was married at twenty-one, a father at twenty-two, divorced at twenty-four. (His daughter, now in her twenties, lives in Boston.) In the mid-seventies, after three years in Florida during which he got a graduate degree in theatre, Sobel found himself again teaching English, now in the suburbs of Washington, D.C. "I determined not to do the school's theatre program because I wanted to audition at the local theatres," Sobel's account continues. "I got a number of small roles, spear carrier and a little better, at the Folger, which was starting its professional life. In my third year in Washington I was substitute teaching and waiting on tables and earning, I think, twenty dollars a week as an apprentice actor.

"That was the point at which I said, Gee, I think I'm going to try acting as a career." Sobel was now in his late twenties. "I took it seriously as a career despite the advice of people who knew what they were talking about. My girl friend of the time came down from New York to do a show. After she saw me in a performance she said: 'God, if you're serious about theatre, there's a lot you've got to learn.' That turned out to be good advice, but it didn't make for a very romantic evening." At that time, Sobel sees in retrospect, he had an excellent background in liberal arts from college and in theatre history from graduate school but still knew little about the practice of acting. When he'd played enough roles to get his membership in Actors' Equity Sobel decided it was time for him to go to New York. "I had a little money set aside and I lived with a cousin in New Jersey. I auditioned and I auditioned, and I didn't get anything, almost nothing. And I wasn't very good. I'd never learned the basic skills. I didn't know what it takes to be a real actor until I was two or three years into running the Pearl."

Unable to find work in his chosen field, and now past thirty, Sobel was at a turning point in his life. "You have a choice. If nobody'll give you work, then you either get out of that field or you find another way. I wanted to do theatre, and I couldn't do it in the job market the way it was. No one would hire me, so I'd just about decided I'd have to hire myself." Now Sobel fell into a directing job that led to his second marriage. Earle Edgerton, an actor and translator he'd met in Washington, asked Sobel to direct a bare-bones production of *Uncle Vanya*. They mounted the show for about three thousand dollars. In the cast was a young actress named Joanne Camp. Like Sobel, Camp was divorced. After an interlude in which he was a director and coproducer at a community theatre in West Virginia, Sobel and Camp were married and he was launching a theatre that would be named the Pearl. After a half season in temporary quarters, the Pearl opened its first season on West Twenty-second Street in the fall of 1984.

Something essential is missing from this account. I say to Sobel that nothing in what he's told me, in the rather aimless person he's described, explains a man who works twice the usual hours for half the pay, and keeps on doing it for seven long years. He laughs rather sheepishly. Finally he says, speaking far more slowly than he usually does: "I'm not sure I know what drives me. My brothers and my sister work as hard as I do." His brothers are, respectively, an orthopedic surgeon and a research engineer. His sister is a physical therapist who specializes in tennis injuries. "The rest of the world does seem a little bit uninspired. I think they're the oddballs, not me." He waves a hand, and goes on: "I'm amazed at how people protect their spare time. I walk down Columbus Avenue and see all these people spending their money in chichi restaurants and cafes. Is that a way to enjoy your life? Night after night? God, how much time do you need to relax? I love to visit friends in the Hamptons, have some drinks with them, but I wouldn't want a place at the beach."

Sobel is silent for a long moment. Then, evidently realizing he still hasn't answered my question, he says almost reluctantly: "I have a notion I'd like to be a part of history, and this is my best shot at doing that. I can have something to say about where theatre is going in the nineties and beyond. I do think theatre can act as a real cure for the ethical and spiritual health of a society. Theatre can do that. It's that important." There is in Sobel, I've learned, an inner voice that whispers to him if something he is saying is beginning to sound at all pretentious. Apparently he's just heard that whisper, because now he leans back in his seat, makes a hands-up gesture much like a shrug, and says: "Beyond that? Beyond that, it's just a Jewish kid from Long Island trying to overachieve."

AUGUST 12

6:30 p.m.: It's a Monday evening. No rehearsal today: Monday is the actors' day off. The Pearl's trustees are meeting to discuss raising money. The topic, always high on the agenda at such theatres, is especially critical in this year of the Pearl's great leap forward.

The Pearl's move up to Off Broadway status will require a very large increase in its budget. Because each show will run for forty-five instead of twenty-four performances, because the actors will be paid more per week for more weeks, because other costs will rise with a longer season—the 1992–93 season will cost $380,000 compared to last year's $251,000. Like most theatres of its size, the Pearl counts on its earned income for only about one half of its budget: $190,000, of which $170,000 is supposed to be earned at the box office if the Pearl can attract enough new audiences for its longer season. That leaves another $190,000 to be raised from foundations and corporations and individuals and sometimes government. That's twice as much as the Pearl's trustees have ever raised. It's a measure of how seriously they take this prospect that already the trustees have voted their first give-or-get requirement: each trustee must raise at least $5,000 or foot the difference.

Discussing how to meet the budget are a dozen people seated in a circle on the bare black stage of the dark theatre. Most of those present are trustees: they are a mixture of business and cultural types who have in common their interest in the Pearl and their ability to raise money. The meeting is run by Ivan Polley, the only person here who spends all his time looking for money for the Pearl. He's employed as its "director of development," the current euphemism for fund-raiser. Polley is a tall, slender man in his early thirties, slightly stooped, with graying hair and a pleasantly low-keyed manner. When we spoke in the spring, Polley said he liked working at the Pearl because of its atmosphere of "we're all in it together" and especially because Shep Sobel was "more human" than other artistic directors he'd worked for. In the year he'd worked there, Polley said, he'd come to think of Sobel as "my friend as well as my boss. I can go to Shep when I'm in trouble."

Polley told me that what was distinctive about the Pearl, its classical repertory and resident company, made it attractive to foundations and some individuals, but not to corporations, which prefer to give to theatres with "splashy names." He was running his first capital campaign when the Pearl set out to raise money for its new home, the larger theatre where, ideally, it would start its tenth season in 1993.

Polley begins the meeting by talking about the capital campaign. "Lots of givers like bricks and mortar, but you have to already have a big chunk of the money in hand," he says, and he adds: "We need to be alert to a naming opportunity." This is a reference to the baptism by money by which so many institutions get their name: Give so much and we'll put your name on a plaque or a seat, but give enough and we'll name the building after you.

He tells us that the spring benefit netted $7,000 for the Pearl. This was a two-performance variety show with tickets at $75. Joanne Camp acted in comic sketches contributed by playwrights in whose plays she has performed. It was the first time I'd seen Camp do comedy: she seemed to enjoy it as much as the audience enjoyed watching her. Alice Tierstein, a choreographer and dance teacher, and also Sobel's cousin, provided two dances, one of them a comic routine she gamely performed with a much younger partner. Polley asks us for money-producing suggestions, and ideas start popping up around the circle on the stage:

"Ask subscribers to give fund-raising dinners."

"Let's try to get more jewelry donated to sell in the lobby." "Does that mean more insurance?" "What I first liked about the Pearl was that I could leave my bag on the seat and know it would still be there."

"Could we sell food in the lobby?" Sobel: "We sell brownies baked by subscribers. Our experience is that comedy sells a lot of brownies. Tragedy doesn't sell brownies."

"How about a high-class T-shirt with actual fake pearls?" Sobel: "We do well on the T-shirts we've got, except that we're stuck with two dozen size-small purples that no one wants."

"How about a raffle for dinner in a neighborhood restaurant?" (More than half the people who attend the Pearl dine in the area—I know this from the survey they took of their audiences.) "Or for a week of theatre in London?"

"How about a seminar at a university, maybe on Saturday morning, with a tie-in to our plays?"

"Every other small theatre I go to makes a pitch for money before the show. Some charming person gets up and does it—it's always soft sell. Why not us?" Joanne Camp speaks for the first time: "I hate that idea. I'd be sad if we did that. A theatre's a temple!" "It's a temple, yes, but we're talking fund-raising."

Camp: "I've seen it at other theatres, and we actors always had to work harder for the first half hour to undo what they'd done to our audience." Sobel: "The last ten minutes before show time is designed to start preparing the audience for the play. I don't want the audience thinking: These poor people, they need money. I'd rather do that in the lobby. I'd love it if there were reliably at every performance two or three people in the lobby to schmooze with the audience about the Pearl."

"How about a brunch with famous people in their apartments?" Sobel: "I feel reasonably violently about appealing to people on the basis of fame." He says this with a smile and in his usual quiet tone, but I know from experience that the suggestion has run aground on one of Sobel's immovable principles. Last spring I asked for some statements by prominent people endorsing the Pearl, assuming there would be a file of flattering quotes. "You won't get any of that from me," he said. I soon learned that Sobel disdains such quotes and does not even circulate favorable reviews. ("The only difference between a critic and anyone else in the audience is that the critic's opinion is printed.") Nothing could be more futile than to argue the issue; he will not be moved an inch. Yet he made it equally clear that he was speaking only for himself. "You can get the quotes yourself if you want," he told me, and he said it without a hint of sarcasm.

Along with the professional fund-raiser, the person most responsible for finding the way to finance Shep Sobel's dreams is Ken Rotman, president of the board of trustees. Rotman is a tall, breezy lawyer in his mid-thirties who currently is running a corporation in downtown Manhattan. His commitment to the Pearl is astonishing. When I phoned him without advance notice at his home on a Saturday afternoon, he talked with me for a full hour and a half. Each time I suggested that maybe I should let him get on with what he'd been doing, Rotman replied that he didn't care about that "when I'm talking about my baby." I asked Rotman how he first got involved with the Pearl. He was a young lawyer in Washington. Between cases he was playing second base on a softball team whose pitcher was married to Shep Sobel's cousin. Rotman had had an early interest in theatre through his mother, a drama teacher. He performed in school plays till eighth grade, when, he said, he gave up acting for baseball.

On moving from Washington to New York, he looked up his pitcher's wife's cousin, attended a couple of shows, became a fan. Then Sobel invited him to a board meeting. Rotman was twenty-nine and new to New York. He felt a lack of social purpose; he wanted to give something back to a world that had treated him better than it treats most people. He went into the board meeting determined to say nothing. He found a group of "arts types." Listening to a budget presentation, he realized that "no one in the room understood cash flow." There was enough money scheduled to come in, but it was so timed that the Pearl would run out of cash in midyear. Rotman broke his vow of silence. A couple of years later he was president of the board. Now he says of his involvement with the Pearl: "I never dreamed it would take so much of my time or that it would be so much fun." Part of the fun is learning how a theatre works. Technical rehearsals—working out the lighting, for example—fascinate him. Rotman is a knowledgeable critic of Pearl performances. Of a newcomer to the company he said: "He's a talented actor, but did you hear that Western accent? We've gotta do something about that!"

Ken Rotman saw some reefs out ahead between here and Sobel's dream theatre. His breezy manner turned sober when he said: "I'll protect Shep's integrity if I can." He's thinking about what you have to do to raise money in the amount needed for the Pearl to have a permanent home in a larger theatre. The easy way to raise a million dollars, Rotman explained, is to sell seats on your board. It's a fact of life in the nonprofit world. In a city where the temples to greed and to art stand side by side, there are a number of wealthy people who'd like to be known for something other than the amount of loot they or their ancestors have stashed away. Membership on a nonprofit board satisfies that side of the ego, and if it's an offbeat place like the Pearl, that gives a rakish twist to the fat cat's whiskers. Sobel may one day have to choose between losing his dream and losing his integrity, and how he approaches that dilemma may put the Pearl's founder at odds with his head cheerleader. How they handle the problems money can buy is far from the least of the questions that may confront them in the coming year.

꒐꒐ AUGUST 13

10:45: Richard Morse is leading the actors through another lesson in movement to the accompaniment of seventeenth-century dance music. "Make that arm beautiful, and make it effortless," he says. "Beauty comes when you make friends with the difficult." Julia Glander, the mime, is moving gracefully, with a rapt expression on her face. She made friends with this kind of movement long ago: she feels at home with it in her body. But others are not finding it an easy friendship. The men especially are still having trouble combining movement and acting. "I can do the style and I can do the lines, but I can't do both," says Dugg Smith. It occurs to me that both Smith and Martin LaPlatney are too big to fit into the style of this time: there just isn't room for men this size in Molière's world.

Morse warns the actors against taking the style too seriously, which will make their movements solemn instead of light and musical. To illustrate, he mimes the three stages of a ballerina's development. First he shows us a child skipping around, happy and graceful. Now she's in ballet school, and her moves are stiff and awkward. At last she's learned her art, and now her movements are once more fluid and also disciplined. His message to the actors, of course, is to avoid getting stuck in the self-consciously awkward second stage. I am once again astonished at how this paunchy middle-aged man can make me see in his heavyset body the nimble form of a young girl.

Morse now suggests moves to three actors that will fit both the style and the sense of the scene they're playing. Frank Geraci's Orgon is telling his daughter, Mariane, why she must take the villain, Tartuffe, as her husband, while the maid, Dorine, is trying to dissuade or derail him by any tactics that come to her agile mind. The essence of the scene is a comic battle for the allegiance of Mariane between Orgon and Dorine, two antagonists who enjoy fighting each other. Morse tells Julia Glander that because of her status as a maid, Dorine is the only one in the household who can move at will in and out of style. Glander, laughing, demonstrates by crossing the room in the graceful curves of the seventeenth century, moving out of it to stamp forcefully on an imaginary bug, then returning once again in style. For the rest of the household, leaving style indicates a crisis important enough to overcome the usual constraints of social conduct. Thus, much of the comic potential for Geraci lies in Orgon's moves in and out of style in his contest with Dorine—moves that are a thermometer of his emotional temperature. He begins by holding his body in the manner of a proper seventeenth-century bourgeois father, and then, when Dorine gets to him, his movements are those of any man exasperated beyond endurance and beyond the bounds of social convention.

The scene lends itself to slapstick and, like slapstick, requires the most precise timing and movement. Orgon is standing at center stage between the two women and turning back and forth like a crazed robot as he tries alternately to lecture his daughter and to silence her maid, who is weaving around taunting him and signaling resistance to Mariane, until at last he loses his temper and aims an ineffectual slap at Dorine. I notice that Geraci aims his slap at Dorine very wide; I find it suddenly touching that he—Geraci, not Orgon—is so obviously afraid he might accidentally hit Julia Glander. Had the slap connected, it could not possibly have hurt this healthy young woman; but the idea of it is far more repugnant, it seems to me, in our day than it would have been a couple of generations ago.

Here Glander invents a marvelously effective movement. She's been inventing moves for Dorine all along, many of which are discarded by Sobel or herself, but this one will remain, in the show and in the memory of many who would eventually see it. Her master has ordered her to be silent, but she goes on giving her reasons why his daughter should not marry Tartuffe:

ORGON: You disregard my orders, is that true?
DORINE: What's your complaint? I'm not speaking to you.
ORGON: Who *are* you talking to?

Now Dorine—the only character who ever shows that she's aware of the audience—turns toward the empty theatre and makes a tentative gesture while looking at the audience that will one day be there with the smile of someone who is sharing a secret. The message could not be more clear: she is talking to *us*. But of course this is just between her and us, so to protect the audience from her exasperated master she pulls back her gesture and replies:

DORINE: To me; that's all.

On the actors' day off I visited Julia Glander at the East Nineteenth Street apartment from which she roller-blades the ten-odd blocks to the Pearl.

I asked her about the day she'd playfully stolen a scene by her way of looking at the other actors while they were talking. She laughed mischievously and recalled that she'd found when playing in the British farce *Noises Off* that a certain gesture always drew a laugh from the audience and that she could repeat it for a second laugh. "It's addictive for an actor," she said. "It's up to the director to stop it."

We went over her marked-up script of *Tartuffe*. Alongside the yellow highlighting of her lines were marginal notes recording the decisions she and Sobel had arrived at about Dorine's thoughts and motives. (There is also a list of words she needs to pronounce or enunciate more precisely when she's in Molière's Paris: "man," "match," "assume," "a*ll* right.")

When she comes on stage to try to help Mariane, Glander notes in the margin: "Assume I'm going to win."

Of her first attempt with Orgon: "Make light of it [his plan to make his daughter marry Tartuffe]."

When Orgon says: "I am getting mad . . ." she notes: "That didn't work."

Of her next attempt, which is to hint that Tartuffe may be interested in Orgon's wealth: "Think of the money! This'll knock some sense into him." But she knows Dorine has made a mistake when she refers to the prospect of a "beggar son-in-law," and Glander writes in the margin: "Oops! Wrong choice of word."

When Dorine makes a frontal attack on Tartuffe as a pious fraud, she says to herself: "Aha! I've got him." But she sees that she's overplayed her hand, and Glander notes: "Oops! He looks pissed." Dorine suggests that a husband forced on his daughter may end with "horns upon his brow," and Glander notes: "Heavy—think of Elmire [Orgon's wife]." And when Dorine goes all out by saying his daughter's sins in that case will be charged to Orgon's account in Heaven, Glander writes: "This is it!"

At last Orgon explodes with "Quiet, you serpent!" And Glander notes for Dorine: "Gotcha!"

Of the moment when Dorine withdraws her lovely gesture to us Glander writes: "Protect audience/don't let Orgon see I'm talking to them."

I asked why none of Dorine's many movements was noted in the margins of the text. "I don't need that," Glander said. "I remember those with my muscles." She said that as she grew into the role she was feeling Dorine in her body more and more. "I love all the physical stuff!" she exclaimed. "Another role might be more bound to the ground, but Dorine lifts, she bounces." Julia Glander bounces too. This attractive, cheerful blonde, who looks something like Wendy Hiller in her early years, is an intensely physical person. "I feel better mentally if I use all my energy," she said. That's a lot of energy. In addition to performing in *Tartuffe*, and because she can't live on what the Pearl can pay, she will be teaching movement to preschool children in her mornings. If there's any bounce left over, she takes a dance class now and then.

Even Glander's humor is physical. It was what I first noticed about her. Whatever else was going on, I was likely to see Glander telling us jokes with her lithe, disciplined body, a physical counterpoint to Sobel's verbal humor. She learned how to tell those jokes early in her acting career: the two years she worked as a mime taught her the clarity and precision of movement that are necessary for roles, like Dorine, which call for a lot of physical humor.

Our talk turned to her career. She started college in Michigan, where she is from, as an art major. A teacher suggested she try out for a play. It was a commedia dell'arte show, and Glander loved both the acting and the miming. She changed her major to acting and for two of her college years she toured with a professional mime performing on campuses and on the streets. She's been acting ever since.

I observed that she seemed to enjoy children and asked if she missed having any of her own: unless you are very lucky, or have a well-to-do spouse, parenthood is beyond the means of an actor. Glander nodded. She was married to a fellow actor for ten years—they were divorced less than a year ago—but they'd never felt they could afford children. She said she feels most keenly the price she's paying for her career when she visits her sister, who has a prosperous engineer husband, three children, and two homes. She said it might still happen to her. (She refuses, smiling, to tell me her age. Her biography suggests she's in her early or mid-thirties.)

Meanwhile, though, she loves her work. It's too hard a life, too hard to make a living at acting, but "I'm doing just what I should be doing." I asked if she felt particularly at home playing Dorine;

of all the actors in *Tartuffe,* Glander offstage seemed to me the most like her onstage persona. At times I could hardly tell them apart; that was true of none of the other actors. Yes, she said, she and Dorine had a lot in common. "We both have a sense of fun, we enjoy mimicry, and we have a lot of drive," she told me. "But we're different in some ways. Dorine's more confident of herself, she's wittier, and she has more street smarts than I do." Glander was smiling. She obviously loved talking about this woman, so like her and yet different, as if she were an admired big sister. Dorine was a happy discovery. Her agent had talked Glander into auditioning for the role, but once she'd become acquainted with Dorine she enjoyed her so much she turned down a better-paying role to stay in *Tartuffe.*

It occurred to me as I was leaving that I'd like to see her in a very different role. "Maybe one day you'll see me play Blanche Dubois," she said, and she laughed at the idea.

꧁ AUGUST 14

Tartuffe is taking physical shape. What began as a group of people reading aloud around a table on a bare stage is displaying the look as well as the voice of Molière's Paris.

The set is up. Now, instead of the passageways leading back-stage and the black cement block of the bathrooms, what I see as I enter the theatre is the interior of a seventeenth-century bourgeois home. I see two walls, slanting away from the orches-tra in a shallow V with its apex at center stage. They are painted peach color, decorated with blue and purple stencils of a branch-like design. I am surprised at how greatly these two painted walls change the mood of the theatre. Without a set the Pearl's interior is strictly a workplace. These two walls with their smiling, elegant colors evoke in me the mood of another time and even a touch of Molière's comic vision. This, I imagine, is what he saw in his mind's eye while he was peopling the stage with the characters of *Tartuffe*.

The set was put up on Sunday, two days ago, after the crew of Richard Morse's one-man show struck their set Saturday night following its last performance. Ours arrived that morning in pieces on a pickup truck from Easton, Pennsylvania, the home of the set builder, who cut its wooden parts from blueprints drawn by its designer. There is a lot of unskilled labor involved in changing sets, and the Pearl sends out a call for volunteers on the two "put-in" days that accompany every new production. Up to a dozen relatives, subscribers, and other friends of the Pearl show up to carry materials in and out, assemble and paint the new set, and help in the myriad jobs that are part of hauling out the old and putting in the new.

I find the set's designer out in the backyard. Robert Joel Schwartz is a round-faced, grizzled man, with the look of an amused teddy bear, who has been doing all the Pearl's sets since its second year. Sobel says twenty-five of Schwartz's thirty-four sets, which he brings in for $300 to $400 a set, have been "fabulous"; they "help the actors perform the play, and the audience receive it." Right now Schwartz is spray-painting a large piece of canvas in the same colors as those of the set. That canvas will cover a table under which Orgon will hide in the climactic scene of the play. "I design around this theatre's deficiencies, which are many," Schwartz informs me between bursts of paint. The biggest design obstacle is, of course, the cement hulk of the notorious bathrooms, which occupies the right rear (stage left, to an actor) of the stage. Now the hulk is veiled by a wall slanted to leave just enough room for a closet that will play an important part in the plot. Schwartz designed the set to have exits at center stage and stage right.

When the actors come on stage to rehearse I see that they are now about halfway into the time of Molière. The costume designer has supplied them with "rehearsal costumes." These are not the costumes they will wear in performance, which have yet to be made, but are outfits roughly from the period, and roughly fitting the actors, that the designer has found in the Pearl's upstairs collection, which is crammed with hundreds of items of clothing and head- and footwear dating from the fifth century B.C. to the early twentieth century. The idea is that while waiting for their own costumes, the actors can start getting used to performing in period clothing.

For the women especially, there's a lot to get used to. I notice first the floor-length skirts that more than all else give women the look of the seventeenth century. (Pleats and hip rolls make the skirts flare out from the body.) I feel a sudden and unexpected sense of loss when I see Julia Glander in a Molière skirt: no longer will I be able to watch her limber dancer's legs flashing with such skilled grace as she moves in style around the stage. Corsets are the novelty that matters most to the actresses who have to wear them. I ask how constricting the corset is. Joanne Camp, an old corset hand, says she's learned how to manage inside it. "It's a matter of where you put your breasts," she tells me. But some of the other women are clearly bothered by this tight wrapping around their chests. Kathryn Lee says the corset makes it hard to control her voice: its pressure forces her voice up from the chest. Julia Glander indicates the weight of the skirt holding her down and the corset gripping her torso, and she asks like a grounded bird: "Now we're supposed to *move*?"

For the men, the novelty is hard-soled shoes with heels. The heels are low, but they affect the wearer's stance by shifting weight forward. This is as it should be for the seventeenth century, when, in the style we've been learning from Richard Morse, you walked on the balls of the feet with the body leading the legs. This too takes some getting used to. In the next days, Dugg Smith would complain of pains in his legs that he attributed to the new heels. Better now than later, of course, which is the purpose of the rehearsal costumes.

For Frank Geraci, the change in his balance is much greater because the designer has provided one-and-a-half-inch heels that will put his Orgon on a par with Joanne Camp, his stage wife.

He tells me he feels "wonderful" in the heels and is grateful for the Morse exercises, without which he might be suffering from cramps in his legs or worrying about his balance. He says the shift in balance will be good for his performance. "It keeps me leaning into everything," he says. "It makes for a more risky, more confrontational performance. I get a heady feeling."

The actors are also getting props from the Pearl's prop mistress. It's none too soon for some of the actors, who've had the problem of what to do with their hands during the play's long speeches, especially when it's someone else's long speech. They're eager to have something to occupy their hands: handkerchiefs for the men, fans for the women. Frank Geraci gets a tricorn hat and a walking stick "to play with." At Joanne Camp's request, Morse demonstrates the code in which a woman could communicate by her fan. No one, however, needs a prop as much as Kathryn Lee, whose Mariane has to stand motionless on stage for long stretches. "Poor Mariane!" Glander said one day, and she had in mind Lee, not her character. Lee herself said she'd never played a role in which she was on stage so much and said so little. Her role constrains her. Unlike the aggressive Dorine, who can always prance around the stage, the demure and timid character of Mariane tends to immobilize the actress playing her. I'd noticed with sympathy how Lee would fiddle with her hands while she stood silently and listened to the others battling over her Mariane's fate. Now she reaches for the fan as if it were a lifesaver.

I am reminded that the actors aren't yet fully costumed for Molière when Kathryn Lee lifts her period skirt to adjust something underneath and I spy her very contemporary jean shorts. And Frank Geraci is still wearing—below his tricorn hat—the T-shirt and long shorts of his pirate outfit. Months earlier I'd listened to the two designers and Sobel discuss the set and costumes of *Tartuffe*. Schwartz and Sobel were in the Pearl's tiny upstairs office next to the costume shop. Barbara Bell, the costume designer, was laid up with an injured back at her home in upstate New York two hours by bus from the city. She joined the discussion on a speakerphone. (It was the first of several design meetings. Next time they would bring preliminary sketches.)

"We're lucky to have these two. They're not your usual Off Off Broadway designers," Sobel told me before the meeting. "They're far more knowledgeable. Barbara knows the painting of the period inside out, and Robert knows the architecture just as well." He was right. I was soon startled by how much the designers knew not only about the time of Molière but about *Tartuffe*. I was struck also by the complex considerations that go into design decisions, and by how efficiently those decisions can be made by skilled professionals who have worked together for years and who know the show, the theatre—and the budget.

Before Bell called in, the others had been discussing the entrances to the set. Sobel described what he wanted for the entrance used by the King's messenger, who brings the news that Orgon is being rescued from his folly by royal edict: "The messenger should come from far away. We see him coming, and the world opens up to him." Schwartz said: "We can aim for an extra level of theatricality." "The play can take that," Sobel said. "Don't fight the fact that we're bringing in an ex machina solution [Molière's use of the King's edict to resolve the plot]." He smiled and added, thinking of how the grim realist of another time would view such a contrived ending: "If it were Ibsen we couldn't finish the play." Bell came on the phone, and Sobel said about the messenger's costume: "We want it to be a knockout—get every sequin in town." But realizing he might cast the actor who plays the messenger in another bit part, he added: "Bear in mind that if he's Monsieur Loyal also, he'll only have thirty-five lines for his costume change."

"Any sense of color?" Schwartz asked, and Bell's voice answered: "None at all." "No pink or green," Schwartz said. "How about pumpkin-brown?" Bell countered: "How about a show in one color?" I'd never met Barbara Bell; I sensed a strong and self-confident person in the voice I was hearing broadcast in Sobel's office. Schwartz observed about her work: "Barbara is interpreting the period, not reproducing it. Whatever she does will be specific to this show, it won't be reproduction by the numbers."

Bell asked Sobel about the date of the play. She observed that *Tartuffe* is usually set very late in the reign of Louis XIV, and that fashions changed greatly over those years. When in the latter half of the century? Anytime in that half century was all right, Sobel said.

About Orgon's wife, Sobel said to Bell: "Elmire takes three hours to dress, but she still has to be free enough to make commedia-style moves." About the maid, who at one point uses her sex appeal on the villain, he said: "The more we're turned on by Dorine's décolletage, the better."

Sobel ended the discussion with another practical thought about the set: "Keep *The Trojan Women* in mind. Don't intrude on their rehearsal space." The point was that the cast of the Pearl's second show would have to rehearse on the set of *Tartuffe*. Theatres like the Pearl can't afford separate rehearsal space.

That afternoon Sobel lectures all of us, actors and ground crew, about the chronic irritation caused by people crossing the small stage while a rehearsal is in progress.

It happens because of the way the Pearl is put together. The only way to get from the front door to backstage, and to the office and costume shop upstairs, is across the stage. By the same token, the only way someone working anywhere backstage can get out of the building is by crossing the stage. Everyone tries to avoid it, but by now half a dozen people are working backstage, and sometimes one of them can't wait to get out. Mary Harpster, the Pearl's general manager, has perfected a technique of slipping across unnoticed, but others are not so skillful.

"Don't cross the stage during rehearsal unless you absolutely have to," Sobel tells the ground crew, and being the person he is, he adds: "But if you have to, try to do it while I'm talking, not the actors." He tells the actors it's going to happen now and then and asks them not to let it disturb them.

Rehearsal resumes. No more than a minute later three roofers emerge from backstage carrying a huge ladder and tromp across the middle of the stage, effectively cutting the rehearsal in two. Sobel briefly throws up his hands, then finds the right commentary on this absurd response to his entreaties. "Do you guys know your lines?" he asks the workmen.

ॐ AUGUST 15

11:00: Two actors are sitting on stage, not in costume, while Sobel is in a first-row seat immediately in front of them. Something new to me is going on.

Sobel is unhappy with the scene between the two lovers, but he doesn't know why it's not working. Either the actors don't really understand the scene, or else they do but are not yet able to express that understanding. This is the scene where Valère comes on stage having heard that Orgon has promised his sweetheart, Mariane, to the villain, Tartuffe. Sobel observes that the lovers are doubly constrained in what they can say, first by the social code of their time, and second by lovers' age-old fear of being hurt by the ones to whom their love makes them so vulnerable. To explore the meaning of the lovers' dialogue more effectively, he asks the actors to paraphrase their own lines and say what they hear in the other person's lines. The scene begins:

VALÈRE. Madame, a piece of news is going about,
Unknown to me, but very fine no doubt.

Arnie Burton paraphrases this as: "I just heard something outside. I need you to tell me it's not true." Kathryn Lee says that Mariane is hearing this as: "Valère knows about father's decision. I want to ask you what you're going to do." As the scene goes on, the growing gap between what the lovers are saying and what they are thinking is evident in Burton and Lee's paraphrasing. Because they respond to the spoken words of pride in each other's lines, not to the unspoken hurt and desire we hear in their paraphrases, the two talk at cross-purposes and soon are quarreling. Valère stalks melodramatically out—"Then, Madame, my last goodbye!"—but is brought back by Dorine, who manipulates the two into a reconciliation. Sobel says he thinks the exercise has advanced everyone's understanding of the scene.

Arnie Burton is the newest member of the Pearl's resident acting company. I spoke with him over lunch months earlier. Burton is a slender, brown-haired man who grew up in a small town in Idaho. His rather innocent good looks and engaging manner make him a natural for young leading-man roles. At thirty-three, he has ten years of experience in the New York theatre. Burton joined the Pearl's company after playing three roles there last season.

For Burton and the Pearl it was love at first sight. It happened when he auditioned for the part of Claudio in *Measure for Measure*. Sobel advised him to "try to affect your partner," Joanne Camp, who was playing Claudio's sister, Isabella. Burton was surprised and pleased by the advice. Actors playing Shakespeare tend to focus on delivering the beautiful lines without conveying to the audience what those lines are saying, which, more often than not, is about what the character wants from someone else on the stage. Both Burton and Camp recalled the simple act of hers in rehearsal that was the key to their scene together. Isabella has come to say farewell to her beloved brother, who is to be executed the next day. The conflict in their goals is stark. She holds it in her power to save her brother by giving herself to the rapist Angelo. Claudio wants her to save him by making that sacrifice: "Sweet sister, let me live." Isabella wants him to accept his doom and so save her from what was then truly a fate worse than death. In the first rehearsals, he'd embraced her when they met. Then one day Camp suddenly and spontaneously spurned his embrace and thereby unlocked in both of them the anger that displaced love as the dominant emotion in their playing of the scene.

For her part, Joanne Camp told me about Burton that she was delighted to find in the newcomer "an actor who trusts himself to go with you if you change the performance." Trust and daring are what this kind of theatre is about: the trust and daring of the acrobat who can let go of her trapeze in an aerial somersault because she knows her partner's sure hands will be there to catch her. Camp said: "You have to keep daring yourself. You have to know your partner will catch you. That's what the audience comes to see. Otherwise they could stay home and watch television."

Burton encountered the Pearl's emphasis on style during his preparation for Arthur Schnitzler's *The Farewell Supper*, which takes place in turn-of-the-century Vienna. To help him see his mistress through his character's eyes, Burton studied portraits of women dating from Schnitzler's time for clues to sexual attitudes. Alice Tierstein, the Pearl's choreographer, coached Burton and Robin Leslie Brown, playing the mistress, in moving in the style of the time by teaching them the Viennese waltz. There's no waltz in the play, but, she said, the dance expresses in movement the flirtatiousness of Vienna's sexual mores. As part of their warm-up before each performance of *The Farewell Supper*, Burton and Brown would waltz on the empty stage, dancing both body and soul into the mood of Schnitzler's Vienna.

After the Schnitzler play, which concluded last year's season, Sobel offered Burton membership in the Pearl company. Now, in the Pearl's backyard, I ask Burton about playing Molière's Valère. Molière is unusually difficult, he says: "The actor has to keep about five balls in the air." In the lovers' scene, for example, Burton has to concern himself with his feelings and motives toward Mariane, but also with moving in period style, with his vocal technique—which still needs work—and with the poetry of the rhymed couplets.

He approached the role by seeking aspects of Valère in himself, and now, in rehearsal, he is finding himself in Valère. Burton says it's hard to convey the intensity and the vulnerability of one who is in love. When he summons his own feelings to help him enter into those of Valère, he draws on his memories of a love affair of four years earlier that was "the best in my life." I ask him how he focuses those emotions on Mariane as embodied by Kathryn Lee. "I see it in her eyes," he says. "I fall in love with Kathryn's beautiful eyes."

Later I ask Kathryn Lee the same question: how does she focus Mariane's love on Burton's Valère? She too starts with the eyes: "I look at his eyes. Arnie has great eyes, and when he's really connected to what he's doing he can bring you into his space. There's a vulnerable thing about Arnie, though I don't know him well enough to know whether it's Arnie or Valère." Like Burton, Lee draws on her own experience of love: "The scene brings to mind my first being in love, my fear of expressing my feelings. I use one memory especially where Valère says he might find someone else. I remember with my very first boyfriend the fear that that might happen, and when it did happen, when he found someone else, the pain of it all. It's an image that works for me."

AUGUST 20

11:15: "Blocking"—the figuring out and recording of the actors' movements on the stage—has begun with the opening scene. The director, of course, decides on the blocking, but it is the stage manager's job to record those decisions. (That record is crucial to the show; often in days to come I'll hear Sobel turn to the stage manager and ask: "What was our original blocking on that?")

I sit by David Waggett to watch him at work. He is at the big homemade desk that squats in a middle row like a giant bug with its short front legs alongside Waggett and its much longer hind legs stretching down to the floor two rows in front of him; the body is the large black board that is the desk's top. I notice that he keeps a double record of the blocking, one in words—"Dorine crosses to stage left"—and another in a diagram recording the same move as a line across the page. His eraser is as busy as his pencil as he tries to keep up with the decisions and revisions taking place on stage; his text begins to look like a battlefield. I marvel at the stage manager's ability to manage all that he is called on to do. At the same time that he is recording the blocking he is also responsible for prompting the actors, who are now "off book": they no longer have their texts in hand but do not always remember their lines. This means the stage manager must keep up with the dialogue on stage in his text. When an actor can't recall what he says next, he calls out: "Line!" and the stage manager must know just where the actor is in the text so he can immediately give him the correct line. He must do it without hesitation, or the actor will lose his rhythm and the stage manager will be blamed. Along with all that, the stage manager must watch the time to call the breaks required by Equity rules. (When I told Sobel how impressed I was with the stage manager's importance, he reminded me that Thornton Wilder made the stage manager, not the director, the narrator of *Our Town*. "That shows what a terrific theatre person Wilder was," he said. Since all this happens in Waggett's presence, I wonder if it doesn't also show what a diplomat Sobel is.)

The opening scene suddenly looks crowded as it never has before. I realize that this is because of the costumes the actors are now wearing. Seven actors, five of them women, are on the Pearl's small stage. The bulky skirts on the five women take up a lot more of that limited space than the actresses themselves do: it is a challenge to figure out how they can move around without colliding and still make sense of the story.

Madame Pernelle, Orgon's mother, is the central figure in this scene. Each member of the household comes on stage, tries to mollify the angry woman, and is roundly denounced by her. Sobel and Anna Minot, playing Madame Pernelle, are calculating her moves in relation to her motives concerning each of the members of the family, and with the others Sobel is working on what they can do when they are not engaged with Madame Pernelle. All this, while staying in the period style—which means they can never turn their bodies in such a way as to exclude one of the others—and without bumping into each other.

Anna Minot and her husband, also an actor, were members of the Pearl's original company. She stopped acting when her husband had a stroke and she had to stay home to care for him. Now he is in a nearby nursing home. Sobel offered her the role of Madame Pernelle because it is challenging without being physically too demanding (she appears in only two scenes). In fact I am impressed by Anna Minot's physical condition. She is long past sixty and is three decades older than the rest of the company except for Geraci. Yet she goes through the physical and vocal warm-ups with the others. I am reminded once again that the actress's body is as essential to her work as her voice: she has to know that she can count on it to do whatever the role calls for. "It's a lot for the muscles to remember," Sobel says about Madame Pernelle's moves in this scene, but Anna Minot's muscles seem well able to handle it.

The scene ends when Madame Pernelle slaps her maid on the way out. "What part of her anatomy do I slap?" Anna Minot asks Sobel, adding hopefully: "I'd rather not slap her face." I notice again, as I did with Frank Geraci's fear of hitting Julia Glander when he aims a slap at her, that a blow that might have passed for trivial a couple of generations ago is now so distasteful to the actor who has to deliver it. The slap remains directed at the face but is reduced to a tap. (The maid is not Dorine, who is more a companion to the daughter, Mariane, than a maid, but a nonspeaking part played by Janine Lindsay, the Pearl's management intern.)

Now we're doing Tartuffe's entrance. The actor making it has to live up to what LaPlatney told me is "the greatest buildup in theatre history. For two acts everyone's been talking about Tartuffe—now at last he's here." LaPlatney's Tartuffe slinks on stage in a long cloak and greasy wig, fingering a crucifix and saying to his servant offstage: "Put back my scourge and hair shirt in their place / Laurent, and pray for Heaven's enlightening grace." Dorine, listening, comments to the audience: "What affectation! What pretentious cheek!" The two fence in a short, sparkling scene. Tartuffe and Dorine are the two street-smart outsiders to bourgeois society and each knows the other is an enemy. LaPlatney and Julia Glander are obviously enjoying the scene: they are two skilled actors with a fine sense of physical comedy. They've both invented gestures that will stick in my memory. Dorine wants to excite Tartuffe in the hope that he will give himself away in his coming meeting with Elmire, so Glander takes a half step toward him, changes expression, and pushes her breasts forward. It's a small gesture, but Glander makes it so precise, and focuses our attention on it so clearly by holding the rest of her disciplined mime's body still, that her usually comic Dorine is all of a sudden very sexy. (In a movie, the camera would direct our eyes to the right place, but on stage it takes the actor's physical skill to do it.) I remember Sobel's injunction to the costume designer: "The more we're turned on by Dorine's décolletage, the better." LaPlatney's Tartuffe responds by reaching out, face averted in pretended modesty, to cover that breast with a hand-kerchief—and while he's at it he tries to cop a feel.

During the lunch break I'm sitting in the sunny backyard with Dugg Smith and Julia Glander. We're talking about changing styles in directing. Not long ago, they agree, the director would lay out the blocking to the actors at the beginning of rehearsal and he would dictate the interpretation of their characters to each of them. No ideas about either blocking or character were asked of or welcomed from the actors; they were not considered capable of such thoughts. All that is changing, they say, and the old-style tyrant is disappearing. Now the director is likely to work everything out with the actors, although inevitably the director has to have the last word. Sobel is, of course, of this second school of directing.

I ask the two actors about the sequence in which scenes are

rehearsed. Instead of staying with a scene till its problems are all resolved, Sobel goes on to the next scene, so that the cast will work through the play half a dozen times. "We have to do it that way because actors can't get all of a scene on the first time around," says Dugg Smith. "Sometimes it comes to you much later, even after rehearsal, during the run of the show. That's when you suddenly say to yourself: That's what it means, that's the way that goes." That's also why actors object to a premature run-through: playing an act, or the whole play, without stopping to resolve problems. The actors aren't ready yet, and in a run-through they have to do things in ways they don't like but haven't yet had a chance to fix.

4:00: We're back on the "Poor fellow!" scene in act I. This is when we first meet Orgon and witness his obsession with Tartuffe in action as he has to listen to Dorine's account of his wife's illness when he only wants to know about his religious mentor. It continues to be one of the hardest moments in the play. "I'm so confused about this scene," says Julia Glander, and that seems to be the mood of the moment.

Frank Geraci is unsure to what extent he should show that Orgon grasps the meaning in what Dorine is saying to him. When she's speaking should he move toward her, indicating a need to know what she has to tell him about his wife? Or stand still because of her lower status in the household? Geraci is also worried about his unresolved questions concerning Orgon. What does Orgon do for a living? Geraci wants to make up his mind about that.

Geraci's mood has swung up and down in the last few days. Ten days ago he told me he was very happy about his Orgon. "My body's started speaking the lines," he said, and this physical taking on of the role was happening much sooner in rehearsal than it usually does. A week later his mood had veered to the opposite extreme. "My Orgon's fragmented," he said. "He's cut up in little pieces, and they're not even in order." I asked him why this had come about. He thought it had to do with his self-consciousness about moving in the period style and his concern with the comedic needs of the moment in each scene. "All I can do now is hang on to the essential character of Orgon," he said.

They start the scene over, but stop after almost every line to discuss it with Sobel. Geraci murmurs "da-da-dum" each time to get himself back into Molière's rhythm. I am in awe once again at what seems to me one of the most mysterious attributes of the actors' art: their ability to slip in and out of their roles so frequently without ever muddying the differences between their characters and themselves.

"Oh shit, this is the one that drives me crazy!" Glander exclaims. "This" refers to Dorine's lines about Tartuffe, and what drives Glander crazy is that she cannot say the lines without the sarcasm that, in Sobel's view, should be evident only in the content, not the tone, of the lines. "Try saying it as if you were talking about someone you like," he suggests. "Put the sarcasm in your looks at Cléante." (Every so often the maid glances over at the brother-in-law to make sure he is registering her master's lunacy.)

Dugg Smith, as Cléante, has to stand by silently during the entire "Poor fellow!" scene. By now he has a crimson handkerchief he uses to occupy his hands. He can hold it because his eventual costume will have no pockets. The costume designer, Barbara Bell, told him that when he consulted her. If he wants to be rid of the handerchief, he can put it up his sleeve or tuck it in his ring, she said.

They move on to another scene. It is clear to me that neither Sobel nor Geraci is happy with the Orgon they are jointly creating. Nor are they happy with each other.

Something is wrong. I sense the changed mood almost immediately when I arrive after missing two days of rehearsal. "Dramatic disgruntlement," Sobel says to me in passing. He doesn't have time to explain.

"Martin and Shep don't see eye to eye on how he's playing Tartuffe," David Waggett, the stocky, bearded stage manager, tells me. I'd noticed that LaPlatney and Sobel were somewhat at odds from the first day of rehearsal; evidently it's getting worse rather than better. "They're not understanding each other," Waggett says. "Martin says, 'I'm doing this,' and Shep says, 'But I'm not getting it.' " I ask Waggett how serious he thinks it is. "It's nothing personal. They're both pros, and they'll work it out. It shouldn't seriously harm the show." That doesn't strike me as a very optimistic forecast. David Waggett, himself a strong-willed, decisive personality, puts part of the blame on Sobel's method of directing. "He's not making himself entirely clear to the actors," the stage manager says. "Maybe it's because of his years of teaching the Pearl actors. He always wants to draw it out of them, but sometimes you have to just tell the actors what to do. Otherwise you leave them confused."

Martin LaPlatney has the same complaint about Sobel's directing. "He's not making clear to me what he wants," he says when I question him between scenes. The tall, strongly built actor is talking more forcefully than he usually does, at least to me. "What I'm doing is comic and in character. Shep doesn't like it but he's not giving me a clear alternative that's equally comic and in character. An actor is often intuitive about the scene. It's dangerous for the director to ignore him."

Disgruntlement is evident in the first scene to be rehearsed. It is the first of the two scenes between Tartuffe and Orgon's wife, Elmire. The villain propositions his patron's wife in a speech that marvelously mixes piety and lust. (He later justifies the combination with these lines: "Yes, now there is a science that succeeds/ In stretching consciences to meet our needs.") Elmire deflects his approach in a manner ambiguous enough so that Tartuffe will renew his attack in the later scene that brings about his downfall. Sobel and the two actors, LaPlatney and Joanne Camp, are trying to mine the comic potential in the scene. At the peak of Tartuffe's tirade, when he declares himself Elmire's "unworthy slave," LaPlatney kneels before Camp and then sprawls on the stage. His size makes it a more melodramatic gesture than it would be in a smaller man. Sobel doesn't like what LaPlatney is doing. "Elmire wouldn't buy that, it's too much," he says. The actor insists that comic excess is right for that moment in the scene. Neither man gives way, and it's clear that much more is at stake between them than the immediate question. LaPlatney shows his mood: he snaps angrily at the stage manager when Waggett's young apprentice doesn't respond fast enough to his call of "Line!"

Now Sobel calls a halt to the rehearsal and he asks LaPlatney to go offstage with him. About fifteen minutes later they return and the rehearsal resumes in a much calmer mood. They strike a compromise on the disputed moment: Tartuffe will kneel but he won't sprawl. I get the impression that both men have decided to pull back from a confrontation over LaPlatney's challenge to the director's authority.

"You see how things are worked out," LaPlatney tells me in the yard later on. "It's all settled for the best." But soon he is again criticizing Sobel's method of directing. He even ventures onto another actor's territory by saying that Sobel is wrong and Frank Geraci right in their latest disagreement about the vexatious "Poor fellow!" scene. I am not surprised when LaPlatney tells me he hopes to move from acting into directing.

Sobel tries to put the incident in perspective. When I talk to him that evening he says: "Martin was testing me. He's asking for respect." As he often does, Sobel sees the other person's behavior in a larger context: "You can't blame him for that—it's hard in this society to win respect when you're forty years old and earning only $180 a week." After a moment he says: "I hope he'll be willing to work my way."

ᖰ AUGUST 25

When I arrive at around 10:30, I'm told in the lobby to enter the theatre very quietly. I tiptoe in and find Sobel alone with an actress who looks to be in her mid-fifties. He is sitting in his usual place in the third row, she is standing on the stage speaking lines whose tragic tone is apparent before I can make out any of the words.

After the actress leaves, Sobel tells me he was auditioning her for the role of Hecuba in *The Trojan Women*, the Pearl's second show of the season, which will go into rehearsal on September 24, twelve days after the opening of *Tartuffe*. Sobel will direct that play also. Directing two consecutive plays plus running a theatre seems a lot for one person. Many artistic directors do not direct any plays; Sobel limits himself to two a season and tries to avoid directing two in a row—just what he is about to do. I ask Sobel if he's spreading himself too thin. He makes a gesture of resignation and says he couldn't get the director he wanted for *The Trojan Women*.

Three of the Pearl's actors will also be working both shows. They'll be rehearsing five hours a day and giving a performance the same evening. What's more, and it seems to me this must make it even harder, they'll have to shift gears back and forth between the French comedy of Molière and the Greek tragedy of Euripides: I can hardly imagine two more different worlds. Sobel explains that these "back-to-back" combinations of performance and rehearsal are essential to meeting the Pearl's budget. During the four weeks of a back-to-back, an actor is paid an extra $50 a week instead of the $180 a week he or another actor would normally earn for the same rehearsal time. That's a saving to the Pearl of more than $500. The season's budget requires Sobel to arrange sixteen back-to-backs. Doing so adds greatly to the complexity of planning a season, for in choosing the plays, he must fit together shows that have a sufficient number of successive roles in which he can cast the seven members of the company. That of course is in addition to finding five plays that he thinks the Pearl can stage and audiences will want to see.

Late in each season Sobel undertakes the task of picking the five plays for the coming year. He works in his upstairs office with, on the wall alongside his desk, a chart showing the plays the Pearl has staged over the last five seasons. He discusses possibilities with Joanne Camp and with Dale Ramsey, the Pearl's dramaturge, but the final decision—and responsibility—is Sobel's alone. "I always have in mind covering the waterfront of classical theatre. I aim for a reasonable selection of periods and countries, and a balance of comedy and tragedy," he told me one day when I was sitting across that desk from him. Sobel follows no rigid rule as to what makes a classic. He asks of a play that it be of sufficient scope to resonate beyond the specifics of its topic and its time and place. He adds, and this is pure Sobel: "The play must delight in language, and it must tell a story, not be an essay divided among a number of people to speak it." So far Sobel hasn't ventured closer to the present than the late nineteenth century.

"This year," he says, "we started with *Tartuffe* to build on our experience with two other Molières and what we'd learned in our workshop in physical comedy. *The Trojan Women* because it's one of the greatest of plays, and because war was on my mind last year [the year of the Gulf War], although we're by no means a political theatre. We do a Shakespeare every year, and by putting *As You Like It* after *Trojan Women* we get six back-to-backs. That schedule gives us a Shakespeare comedy for the holidays, and that seems right. Then Ibsen's *Ghosts* because I think with our new contract we can attract the right actors for it. We'll end the season with four of Chekhov's one-act comedies. We missed the farce in *Uncle Vanya* and I want us to practice Chekhov comedy before we do any more of his plays." I found out that choosing plays involves still other criteria when I asked Sobel if he ever considered doing Shaw's *Saint Joan*. He smiled and answered that *Saint Joan* has a scene with "about fifty people on stage"—far too many for the Pearl's space—and has only one part for a woman: four of the seven members of the Pearl's company are women. He said he has to rule out many classics because they don't have enough female roles.

11:00: Sobel and three actors are sitting in the first row and on the edge of the stage. Sobel is in his usual jeans, and the actors are out of costume and back in shorts. They all have their texts in hand along with a pen or pencil. They're doing something Sobel calls a "spine-through." This is an exercise intended to sharpen their focus on the play's line of action—its spine. "What you know isn't showing in the scene," he says. He tells the actors the spine-through will fix the line of action more clearly in their minds. Geraci briefly objects: "I want it in my body, not my mind." "It'll only take six minutes," Sobel answers mildly, and he goes on. He asks each of them to say, using only Molière's words, what needs to be emphasized in their lines to carry the action to the next person:

> DORINE: Well, have you lost your tongue completely, Miss?
> And *do I have to play your part in this?*
> Let him propose a project that absurd,
> And not combat it with a single word!
> MARIANE: *What can I do?* My father is the master.
> DORINE: *Do anything* to block such a disaster.
> MARIANE: *What?*
> DORINE: *Tell him you can't love just on his whim;*
> That you are marrying for yourself, not him.

"You must give the other person something to do," Sobel tells them. "Sometimes it's hard to decide what's most important to stress, but it's going to make a big difference in how your scene partner responds." As an example he tells Arnie Burton that what he emphasizes in these lines of Valère would determine how Mariane answers him in her following lines:

VALÈRE: What? Would you have me foster in my breast
The love that, when you wanted, you possessed?
Am I to watch you seek another's arms
And not console my heart with other charms?
MARIANE: No, that's exactly what I want. Alas!
I wish it had already come to pass.

If Burton stresses Valère's first two lines, Mariane's reply encourages him to remain faithful to her, whereas if he emphasizes the thought in the last line, she will be telling him—with the same words—to find another lover.

By this stage in rehearsal the difference between one reading of a line and another is sometimes so subtle as to escape me completely. Of course Sobel and the actors—like dogs registering sounds too high for human ears—are able to hear what I miss. As I think about this, I realize that most members of the audience wouldn't be able to tell the difference any better than I, but that the sum total of many such imperceptible shifts in emphasis can determine whether the play reaches the hearts of the audience. They may not know why, but they'll know whether the play moved them or not.

Now Sobel adds a prop to the exercise to make what he calls a "sponge-through." This time the actors speak all their lines, not just those highlighted in the spine-through. "We're not making enough demands on our partners," Sobel says while introducing the exercise. When an actor reaches the words in his lines that make a demand of any kind on another character, he tosses the sponge supplied by Sobel to the actor playing that character. That actor responds by tossing the sponge—and the verbal ball—to the character on whom *his* lines make a demand. "Throw the sponge back if the person's not making a convincing enough demand on you," Sobel asks. "And grab for the sponge if you're insisting on something." His purpose, again, is to sharpen the actors' focus on the demands they are making, to get them with the toss or grab of the sponge to push that demand more emphatically on the other actors, with their muscles as well as with the voice. The actors laugh as they fling the sponge around among them, and at one moment Tartuffe and Dorine are wrestling for it, but they are also utterly serious about making their moves in the spirit of the play. As I watch them enjoy themselves at work, I realize once again that there is a lot of fun in this painfully difficult profession.

During a ten-minute break I seek out Joanne Camp to ask about the results of her daily vocal exercises. She tells me the actors are successfully increasing their vocal range in the exercises, but she's not sure how much of that is carrying over to their work on stage. One actress still has a tendency, as did Camp when she was younger, to get shrill and nasal in the upper register, and one of the actors is still running out of breath in his long speeches. Because of the demands of her own role in *Tartuffe*, and her many administrative duties, she doesn't have time to work with the actors individually on their vocal problems. In this as in so many other ways, there is never enough time.

The stage manager agrees. David Waggett says he notices that the actors' vocal ranges have expanded since the exercises started two weeks ago, but that in some cases the improvement does not carry over into rehearsal. Waggett thinks Sobel—and Molière—are asking too much of the actors. They are trying to learn movement style from Richard Morse, and now they are starting to block their moves on stage. First and always, of course, they have to make sense of the words. It's all necessary, and there isn't enough time for it all.

6:00: Sobel is sitting in one of the middle rows listening to some lively taped music. With him is a short, compact young woman with light brown hair whom I recognize to be Donna Riley, the sound designer for *Tartuffe*. We're listening to selections she's proposed for the half hour of music Sobel wants to be heard in the lobby before the show. Riley has chosen French baroque, music of the seventeenth century, mostly by François Devienne, that might have been performed in those of Molière's plays that were accompanied by music. (*Tartuffe* was not one of these.)

In recent days I'd noticed Riley sitting silently in the back of the theatre watching the actors rehearse. Today, while waiting for Sobel, she chatted with me about her work. She spoke of her craft with such quiet confidence that I was surprised to learn she'd just graduated from the North Carolina School of the Arts with a degree in sound design. She was, she told me, a theatre person who decided she wanted a career in sound design after some years of acting and working backstage as an electrician and as a sound operator. In the latter job she carried out the instructions of the sound designer she has now become.

Riley expected she would be at the Pearl for about twenty days, though seldom for full days, before her work ends on the day the show opens. For this she will be paid $270; she is designing two other shows at the same time. Riley designed *Tartuffe* after Sobel had told her what he wanted. "Some directors dictate to you, but not Shep," she told me. "He gives me plenty of leeway. He says to me, 'This is the feeling I want,' and leaves it up to me to suggest ways to get there." Much of her work involves sound effects, she said, but in *Tartuffe* there will only be instrumental music. The preshow music will run more than thirty minutes to allow for late starts, she said, and the intermission music can go beyond its allotted ten minutes for the same reason. The music between Molière's acts, when there will be no intermission, will run just thirty seconds.

The tape of Riley's preshow music comes to an end. Sobel sits silent for a moment, then nods and smiles. "That's good," he says. Donna Riley packs up her kit of tapes and cassette player and leaves saying she'll be back with the rest of the music.

11:00: "It's wet-noodle time!" announces Julia Glander. She's leading the daily style warm-up, and she wants the actors to shake themselves as bonelessly as their bodies will allow. Sobel has changed the format of the warm-up so that the actors are practicing how to enter and exit in the highly stylized manner of the period. The actors appear in the doorway, making sure to get that lift in the chest as they first look across the stage, and when they exit they must be careful to leave gracefully without turning their backs on anyone, especially anyone of equal or greater social standing.

11:50: We're starting once more at the beginning, the opening scene when Orgon's mother, Madame Pernelle, battles the entire family. Sobel's primary concern now is movement; I notice how smoothly he himself moves as he demonstrates what he wants from them. The entrances the actors have just been practicing are especially important here as the members of the family come on stage one by one for their confrontation with Orgon's angry mother: it is their introduction to the audience. Sobel instructs each actor to enter, pause for a second in a motionless posture, then move in such a way as to relate to Madame Pernelle. He has them counting the beats from their entrance till they reach their place on the stage. During much of the scene, when Madame Pernelle is denouncing the members of the family in turn, five of the seven people on stage have no lines. Sobel stresses one of the most basic, and all too often ignored, rules of stage presence: "You must pay constant, physical attention to whoever is speaking. How can we expect the audience to listen if the other actors aren't listening?"

We move on to the difficult "Poor fellow!" scene. It still isn't working. Neither Sobel nor Frank Geraci likes what Geraci is doing. Sobel tries reducing the visual comments made by Dorine—her miming behind Orgon's back—but that doesn't seem to help. "I can't find the focus," Geraci says. As always he has been imagining the circumstances that would explain his character's behavior. Most recently he's been thinking about Orgon's relationship to the maid, who in this scene is trying to tell him his Tartuffe is a phoney. "I'm nouveau riche, only one generation away from Dorine," he speculates. "Subconsciously I know she's right, and I want her approval." But all that does not add up to a way to do the scene, and Geraci has a special reason for being concerned. "There's a danger the director will impose his conception if I don't find mine, and I don't want that, not with this director," he tells me.

3:00: Sobel is on stage with Hank Wagner, who is the youngest member of the cast. He is a slight, scrawny figure, cheerful, and sometimes so boisterous that he seems younger than his twenty-two years. Wagner is playing the small but crucial role of Damis, the hotheaded son of Orgon. Sobel scheduled this time to work alone with him after the young actor stopped in the middle of rehearsal, turned to Sobel, and said: "I'm sorry, but I feel ridiculous."

The mood on stage is different from that of the other rehearsals I've observed, and not just because Sobel for the first time is working with a single actor. It's not in his nature to be harsh with anyone, but his firm and gentle manner in directing Wagner seems to me as parental as it is professional. Most of his instruction seems intended to calm the young man's intensity. "Don't try to do five things at once, two is enough," he says, and: "Start low and let it build. The anger's in the words—you don't need it in the voice."

Sobel and Joanne Camp, who have no children together, do in fact stand in loco parentis to Wagner, who first came to the Pearl when he was a troubled teenager attending New York's High School for the Performing Arts. Wagner grew up in the tough and alien environment of Spanish Harlem, moved upstate with his mother when his parents parted, then returned to the city to live with his father, go to high school, and try to become an actor. It was his second career as a performer. In his early teens he'd been a boy soprano "earning good money" singing at the Cathedral of St. John the Divine. He switched to acting as a goal, he said, because he knew his singing career would end when his voice changed. He lost his way in high school in the big city. "I was a high-strung kid," he recalled. "I was doing a mess of drinking and drugs"—he was only sixteen—"and not much schoolwork. I only got by because the standards at Performing Arts were so low."

He came to the Pearl at the suggestion of Dale Ramsey, the Pearl's longtime dramaturge, who worked in publishing with Wagner's father. "Dale told me if I was interested in acting I might as well spend the time I wasn't going to school at a real theatre instead of wasting it on the street," Wagner recalled. So in his last two years of high school the youth spent much of his time at the Pearl helping out in the myriad odd jobs that need doing at a small, struggling theatre. That's where he'd learned the handyman skills that are now so useful to the Pearl in Wagner's other role as an assistant stage manager. There, too, he found in Sobel and Joanne Camp a second set of parents, and, with their help, he regained his bearings. When he finished high school, they advised him to go to England for his schooling in theatre. "There you'll have a clean slate," Sobel told him. After three years at London's Central School of Speech and Drama, and recently married, Wagner returned to New York and came around to the Pearl.

Sobel offered him an internship at rock-bottom pay—$75 a week—for which he would get a few parts and earn some of the stage credits he would need to become a member of Actors' Equity. (Since Equity requires membership for all but a few ill-paid roles, and since most New York theatres follow its rules, acceptance by Equity is essential to a stage career.) "Joanne told me not to let myself become one of those well-trained actors who's working in a restaurant," Wagner recalled. "At first my ego was too big, but my wife told me to take it, and I did." That was last year. This season Wagner is listed as an "acting apprentice" and assistant stage manager, is working fifteen or more hours a day—as long hours, almost, as Sobel himself—and is paid $125 a week.

Camp and Sobel almost had their own child last year. Her first pregnancy at the age of thirty-nine came as a welcome surprise. She'd always assumed that she could never bear children. The couple figured out that, by careful management of their time, they could raise a baby while they were running a theatre. Then miscarriage ended their planning.

Children are notable for their absence in the world of the Pearl. None of the seven members of the acting company is a parent, nor are any of the ground crew, with the exception of Sobel himself, who has a grown daughter from his brief first marriage. It's how women in theatre most notably deviate from the social role in which they were cast at least until recently. Just as men were supposed to make money and marry, women were supposed to marry and bear children: at the Pearl, and in the theatre generally, neither sex lives up to society's expectations. And when actors do become parents, economic necessity often forces them to leave the theatre. As Sobel noted in one of his annual reports, seven of the eight actors who left the company in one season became parents within a year before or after their leaving.

Camp and Sobel haven't given up, not quite. "It could still happen," Sobel says, but then he adds: "The chances get smaller every year. In five years I'll be fifty, Joanne'll be however many years younger. [Camp, who unlike most actresses doesn't conceal her age, will then be forty-five.] I think we'll be sorry if it doesn't happen. I'll say: 'That's something we should have done.' "

10:30: We're devoting today's rehearsal to the two scenes between Tartuffe and Elmire. The second of these, the table scene, is the fulcrum on which the plot turns. This is when the villain betrays himself. The actors and director have worked on these scenes several times over the three weeks of rehearsal but are still dissatisfied.

What's going on is a sexual duel with the allegiance of Elmire's husband, Orgon, as the prize. The two are worthy antagonists. As Joanne Camp observed to me, "Tartuffe and Elmire are the two cleverest people in the play." In the first scene, Tartuffe is trying to bed his patron's wife. In the second, Elmire uses his lust to trap him.

Sobel is discussing Tartuffe's approach to his prey with Martin LaPlatney: "You've done it before, this is a sales job. Tartuffe is an operator. He's experienced and he's good at what he does. You want to give him an air of being in control until his lust makes him lose that self-control."

Much of today's time is spent on two moments that turn on how the actors move. Here the director and actors are truly creating the play. Neither moment is spelled out by the author. Molière tells us that the movements occur, but not how, and the how is where their meaning lies: how the actors move helps to define for us the people they are portraying.

"Let's sit down, here is a chair," says Elmire. Tartuffe brings up a chair that's a dozen feet away and sets it close to Elmire's. How does he do it? There are many possibilities. He can bring it all the way across the stage in one bold lunge, or in many short, tentative moves stretched out over several lines, or he can do anything in between; and each choice will say something different to the audience about Tartuffe. LaPlatney tries a number of ways of moving the chair, and the others consider each both for its comic potential and for what it says about Tartuffe's approach to Elmire—how fast is he moving in on her?

A bit later Molière's stage direction reads: *Puts his hand on her knee.* Then:

ELMIRE: What are you doing with your hand?
TARTUFFE: Feeling your gown: what soft, velvety stuff!
ELMIRE: Please don't, I'm very ticklish. That's enough.
(*She moves her chair away.*)

Sobel and the actors discuss what is going on in the minds of Tartuffe and Elmire at that moment. To LaPlatney he suggests: "Tartuffe is inquiring how receptive she is to his advances." How receptive *is* she? She doesn't, after all, pull away immediately. Does this Elmire—Joanne Camp's Elmire—enjoy the man's hand on her thigh? Does she take a moment from her stated purpose in the scene, which is to dissuade Tartuffe from marrying her stepdaughter, Mariane, for a bit of sexual pleasure? Or does this Elmire let the hand linger because she is consciously luring him on, which means she has already decided on the trap she will eventually set for him? The questions are raised but they are not answered today.

After a break, we move on to the table scene, also between Tartuffe and Elmire. (Orgon is hidden under the table, but since he doesn't emerge or speak till the next scene, Frank Geraci doesn't have to be there for this rehearsal.) In the interim Elmire has come to realize that only she can save the family from her husband's blind devotion to Tartuffe. She challenges Orgon to hide under the table and witness what his hero does when he's alone with his patron's wife. Orgon grudgingly agrees. She sends for Tartuffe. Dorine, dubious, says he "may not be so easy to outwit." But Elmire is confident of the power his desire gives her: "Oh, no! A lover is not hard to cheat."

"This scene is going to change quite a bit, but without losing any of the good stuff [that they'd decided on in earlier rehearsals]," Sobel starts off. "We have to build suspense. We've been leaping at the conclusion." The suspense lies in whether Elmire will succeed in luring Tartuffe into revealing himself before her husband. Sobel agrees with Dorine that Tartuffe is too smart to be easily caught, so "it'll take much longer before he gets on top of her." Sobel is not thinking of any change in Molière's text: at the Pearl, the author's words are sacred. But Molière doesn't tell us when Tartuffe, his suspicion overcome by his lust, actually tries to climb on top of Elmire (on the table and therefore over her concealed husband). By delaying that move Sobel is delaying the moment we know that Tartuffe has come to believe her invitation is genuine—that he's fallen into her trap.

The scene is physically difficult for Joanne Camp. She's in costume now, which means the corset and a dress with multiple skirts. While wearing all that, she has to sit on the table, half reclining, her feet on a chair, and, in that position and in the constricting corset, she has to manage her voice and body as she delivers her seductive invitation to Tartuffe. I think she must be terribly uncomfortable, but, always a good soldier, she never complains except to observe that "this dress weighs a ton and a half."

She does complain, surprisingly, about her husband's direction. For the first time in my experience, they are not communicating. "I'm not sure what you want," she says, when he is "fine-tuning" her opening lines, and later in the scene: "I know what you're saying, but I don't know how to do it." She is also dissatisfied with the emotion that underlies her performance. "I'm not aware of Orgon [under the table on which she is sitting]," she says. "He could be dead down there." In fact, of course, Orgon—that is, Frank Geraci—is *not* down there; he's not even in the theatre. But Camp is unwilling even in his absence to rehearse the scene without summoning the feeling Elmire has about her husband while she is seducing Tartuffe. It is also characteristic of Camp that she volunteers this self-criticism without any suggestion from her director or scene partner.

Sobel stops the rehearsal for a three-way discussion of the scene. They talk calmly, without histrionics, and I get no sense of two-against-one, either the actors against the director, or the Sobels against Martin LaPlatney. But though the conversation is reasonable, it is soon evident that it hasn't accomplished its goal.

Camp and LaPlatney now run through the table scene without interruption. "Is that okay?" Sobel asks. "I think so," Camp says dubiously. "I think so," echoes LaPlatney, also dubious. None of the three sounds convinced that the scene is working. The rehearsal ends on that uncertain note.

This afternoon Martin LaPlatney is excused to audition for a commercial. It's a fact of life for theatres such as the Pearl. Equity rules require the theatre to give an actor time off to audition for and make television commercials. (Equity also allows an actor to break his contract and leave the theatre during the run of the show if he gets a better-paying offer elsewhere.)

"Actors' lotto," LaPlatney tells me as he is leaving for the audition. Commercials are indeed a rare opportunity for an actor to make a lot of money for very little work. Serious actors like those at the Pearl see commercials as a way to raise their standard of living at least temporarily while they do live theatre at starvation wages. So I often hear them talking about commercial auditions and how well so-and-so is doing with an ad for such-and-such.

It works like this. The actor will be paid for making the commercial (the audition is unpaid) a minimum fee of $414 for an eight-hour day of "on-camera" work or $313 for a "voice-over" (in which the actor is heard but not seen). A commercial provides the actor one or two days of work, seldom more. Also—and here is the lottery—the actor will be paid a royalty, known as a "residual," each time the commercial is shown on television. If shown on a network program, the rate starts at $40 per showing, then drops to $20. This is in a thirteen-week period. If the advertiser wants to use the commercial after that, he must pay the actor another fee, as if he were making it again, and another round of residuals. These residuals can run to tens of thousands, and sometimes even hundreds of thousands, of dollars. As in a lottery, winning is a matter of luck, or so actors I know will say. You're more likely to be cast in a commercial "because you look like Uncle Ricky," in LaPlatney's phrase, than because of any acting talent you displayed in the audition. But, again as in the lottery, losing happens more often than winning, even for one-time winners, and actors are full of stories about colleagues who were making a lot on commercials one year and now are once again poor.

The woman LaPlatney lives with is one of the lucky ones. Susan Greenhill and LaPlatney are both serious actors who want above all to do live theatre. Both work fairly regularly, usually at theatres like the Pearl, sometimes out of town in the better-paid Equity category known as "regional theatre." They teach acting classes together. Neither is a star, and, in mid-career, neither is likely to become one. In most occupations, they would be considered relatively successful at their work and would earn a comfortable living. But their income as serious actors is both meagre and precarious.

The difference in this household is that Susan Greenhill frequently makes commercials. Although, in 1991, she made a film and appeared in a soap opera, as well as two serious plays, two-thirds of her income was earned in the few days she spent making commercials. Or, from LaPlatney's point of view, one day's commercial brings in more than his pay for two *weeks* of *Tartuffe*. And that's why he carries the other actors' good wishes with him as he goes to his audition.

That evening around sunset, after the others have gone, I am with Sobel in the by now familiar setting of the Pearl's modest backyard. I sit down with some trepidation, but the creaky metal chair holds up for one more conversation. It's a pleasant time of day in August in the city: past the heat of noon, still warm enough to sit under the darkening blue sky in short-sleeved shirts. Sobel, however, seems harried and out of sorts. He apologizes for his mood and says he is willing to submit to my questions. If he is bored, or would rather be doing something else, he will not let me see it: that would not be in the personal style of this man who faces the world with the grace and courtesy you'd expect in a Molière drawing room.

With the day's rehearsal in mind, I ask if the fact that he is married to Joanne Camp contributes to the tension between himself and Martin LaPlatney. Yes, he says, in the sense that a marriage between the director and an actor always creates problems, especially for the other actor, who, knowing that his scene partner goes home every night with the director, may feel himself to be the odd man out. It does not trouble him to direct Camp in love scenes. "I've directed her in scenes where she is the sexual aggressor, much more so than here," he says. But the continuing problem with LaPlatney does trouble Sobel. He says: "Sometimes I wonder, can I handle strong male actors in their forties?" I note in passing that the description fits Sobel himself.

With three of the four weeks of rehearsal spent, I ask, what is left to be done? A lot, Sobel says, and he lists the unsolved problems of *Tartuffe:* "We have a lot of integrating of movement and language to do. We need to clean and clarify our moves, our pivots and turns and postures. The differences in movement style among the actors are far too great." I ask which scenes most disturb him. "The two scenes between Tartuffe and Elmire"—the ones just rehearsed that day—"they're the worst. The 'Poor fellow!' scene and also the one after it, one-five [the scene between Orgon and his brother-in-law, Cléante]. We haven't cracked them either." Those are the scenes led by Tartuffe and Orgon, and Sobel says he still has "continuing differences" with the two actors playing those roles, Martin LaPlatney and Frank Geraci.

Are we behind? Yes. Is Sobel worried, I ask, though the answer is written on the usually cheerful landscape of his face. "We don't have enough time. We could use another three weeks of rehearsal." Sobel says that four weeks is an awkward length, too short for a portrait in oils and too long for a pencil sketch. We recall the story about Stanislavski's invitation to direct a play in the United States. How long did the master need for rehearsal? Two years, Stanislavski is supposed to have said, but if he couldn't have that, two weeks would be plenty. Sobel agreed. In a short rehearsal period, the director decides everything: he interprets their roles for the actors and he blocks all their moves. "It's amazing what you can do in a week or two in summer stock," he says, "and no one ever asks about motivation." I ask if Sobel himself ever directed that way. Yes, he said, years ago, when he was directing student productions in high school and community college. But he doesn't want to work like that with the talented professionals at the Pearl.

As Sobel sees it, his job as director is to help the actors explore their characters and then to stand in lieu of the audience and tell them if what they are doing is working. "The director never knows the character better than the actor, but because he stands outside the actor's skin he can tell him how his performance is coming across the footlights and how it fits with what the other actors are doing." Actors have varying needs. Sobel uses two Pearl actors (neither is in *Tartuffe*) to make the point. "Robin is her character right down to her toes, but she has little directorial eye. She needs the director to tell her how it's reaching the audience. Stuart, on the other hand, does have a director's eye. He knows just what he's doing to the audience. What he sometimes needs is to be pushed to dig deeper into his emotions and make his performance resonate more deeply."

Beyond his work with the individual actors, the director must interpret the text to the cast so that the actors' multiple images of the story are fused into a single vision. He also coordinates the physical aspects of the production: the set, the costumes, the lighting, the sound. While Sobel was describing the function of the director, I'd at first thought the best analogy was to the conductor of an orchestra (though, of course, the director doesn't appear on stage) who fuses the many voices of the instruments into a single statement. Now I see a better analogy in my own field. The editor of a newspaper or magazine must be much like the director of a play: he helps the writer define the assignment, he edits the result, and he makes sure two writers don't contradict or repeat each other. In both professions there's been an evolution from the legendary tyrants of yesterday to the relative democrats of today. And, remembering from my own experience the tyrant's saving grace, that when it goes wrong it's not *my* fault, I think I better understand those actors who say they are more comfortable with yesterday's directors.

Returning to *Tartuffe*, Sobel says: "What I have to aim for now is the best production I can get with this company in this time. I can't pursue the ideal production." I hear a wistful note in his voice: "But if I had a company with five years' experience of Molière . . . " That, of course, is Sobel's dream. It is the theatre in which the actors are so fully trained in classical movement and speech that when they go into rehearsal they are free to devote all their attention to the content of the play. It is the theatre where the actors tune their instruments every day with movement and vocal workouts as surely as the dancer does his daily exercises. This season Sobel is attempting a long stride toward that eventual goal. Whether the Pearl succeeds with its first production of the season, the *Tartuffe* we are now rehearsing, is the most pressing question before him.

AUGUST 31

11:00: All eleven members of the cast are on the stage. They are sitting around in their twentieth-century casual attire. Sobel is in his usual seat in the third row.

Sobel is again trying to speed up the performance. He asks the actors to stress in each passage the news they are bringing—the part of each speech that moves the story ahead. The actors deliver the lines as they always do, but they add just a shade of emphasis to the critical words. The point of the exercise, Sobel tells me, is to help the actors—and eventually the audience—to focus on the story line. "It gives a sense of forward movement," he says, and after a moment's reflection he adds: "I'd like that to be my trademark."

Julia Glander mimes the effect of the speed-up, with a mischievous grin, by patting her head and rubbing her stomach.

During the lunch hour Sobel is at the stage manager's desk looking over the blueprints of the set for *The Trojan Women*—a reminder that the first rehearsal for the next show is only three weeks away. When I get a moment with him, I ask Sobel about an error in the translation of *Tartuffe*. (The Pearl is using a recent translation by the late Donald M. Frame of Columbia University.) Two French speakers in the ground crew have pointed out to Sobel that the word "inherit" is used where the meaning of the French is "acquire." It occurs when Orgon is telling Tartuffe that he is giving him all his worldly goods, including his home. Tartuffe then evicts Orgon, which he obviously could not do if he were inheriting rather than acquiring the property. I tell Sobel I thought I heard "inherit" during the morning rehearsal. Yes, Sobel says, he left it in because he couldn't find a satisfactory substitute. He tells me not to worry: the actors will speak the lines in such a way that the audience will not be misled by the misused word. I am not sure just what that means, and indeed I suspect Sobel of putting me on, but as it works out no one ever complains of being misled by the offending word.

This afternoon the cast runs through the play once again. "What I'm anxious to keep is the barreling tempo you had this morning," he tells them. During the run-through Colleen Davis, the apprentice stage manager, is there text in hand to answer the actors' call of "Line!" Only four times does an actor call for a line; they have pretty much committed their lines to memory (though, inevitably, one or another will flub a line sometime during the run).

When Sobel talks to the actors after the run-through, their positions are reversed. The actors are sitting in the orchestra,

Sobel is standing on the stage. He is making brief, detailed comments, known in the trade as "notes," which he addresses to each actor's character:

"Madame Pernelle, you need to be further upstage—go on a plane with Elmire."

"Dorine, let Orgon breathe before you interrupt after the turn—it makes a better bit."

"Mariane and Orgon, try to cover two more steps coming downstage."

"Elmire, skip the middle beat before 'I'll go up.' "

"Valère and Mariane, never stop to think!"

"Orgon, just one turn on 'Traitor!' "

At the end of the day Sobel says to the actors: "All that's missing is color and variations. Your personalities will add a lot when you make it yours—and the play is crying out to be yours."

SEPTEMBER 1

9:00: The Pearl's tiny lobby is so cluttered I can hardly get past the door. The speaker's stand that serves as the box office, the coatracks, the coffee machine, all are piled along with other odds and ends in the middle of what little space the lobby has, and covered with drop cloths while Hank Wagner paints the walls and ceiling. Dressed in painter's coveralls and cap, Wagner is up on a ladder plying his roller. I notice that the normally boisterous young man seems downcast. When I point this out to him, he gives me an abashed look and an explanation.

Last night, after rehearsal, Wagner was painting the corridor that winds from the stage past the dressing rooms to the back-yard. He stepped on a pan and spilled paint on the new carpeting that he and Sobel had, two days earlier, spent many hours cutting and fitting and installing. It took the two of them far into

the night—the Saturday night of Labor Day weekend—to remove the spoiled carpeting, clean up the mess, and install a new
section. Such times try men's souls, so I immediately ask if Sobel
lost his temper. "Not Shep, never," the young man says. "But he
couldn't laugh about it till this morning."

Today is Sunday of Labor Day weekend, when any New
Yorkers who can afford it, and some who can't, are out of the city
or at the very least are not at work. But all the actors, and with
one exception all the Pearl's ground crew, are here to help get
the theatre ready to receive its first audience of the season at
Thursday's dress rehearsal. The exception is Ivan Polley, the tall,
soft-spoken fund-raiser whom I haven't seen since mid-August.
I'm told he was on vacation and then fell ill with the flu.

I ask Mary Harpster, the Pearl's general manager, why she is
here. She is a Wellesley graduate in her late twenties who is
starting her fifth season at the Pearl. Why on this day is she here
sweeping floors and sewing costumes—among many other odd
jobs—while her contemporaries and classmates are lolling on a
beach in the Hamptons?

"Well, it *is* called Labor Day," she jokes, and then she says: "I
talk to my friends from school who went into banking or Bloom-
ingdale's and they all hate what they do. They're not interested
in the products of their work. I love my work. I'm working in a
place with people who want to be there, and we're working for
a common goal that in some way makes the world just a little bit
better." As I listen to her I'm taken back to the mid-sixties when
I was interviewing young Americans serving in the Peace Corps.
Many of them had set out to save the world; by the time I visited
them in some forgotten corner of Africa they were content to
hope they could leave that corner just a little bit better.

Like other members of the ground crew, Mary Harpster does
not experience the actor's thrill of commanding the audience's
response; she knows instead that she helps to make it happen. In
fact, she makes it happen as much as anyone except Sobel
himself. She is his administrative alter ego, the indispensable
person who keeps track of everything. "I do everything Shep

doesn't want to do" is one version of her job description. That means most of the day-to-day administration of the theatre, and it is difficult to describe. "Funny thing about this job, I'm busy all the time but it's hard to tell you what I do all day. I come in around ten-thirty, and I go home at eight, and Bruce [Harpster, her husband, who is an actor] asks me what I did today. I say: 'Well . . . ' I spend a lot of time talking to people, keeping them happy. I collect the money in the mail and the box office and I pay the bills and I deal with fire inspectors and vendors and creditors. I don't particularly like administration, but I like getting things done. I don't really care what I'm doing so long as I'm in control of it and it's running smoothly."

More than most people here, Mary Harpster is aware of the great difference between this and the Pearl's previous seasons. "I could see the sense of pride in the company members when I handed them their first Equity contract," she recalls. (As an Off Off Broadway company, the actors worked without a contract.) "Now they get a weekly check for the first time, with all the deductions. It feels more like part of the real world, less like something on the edge. We're going to do a lot more theatre here. We're starting the season a month earlier, and we're doing shows six days a week instead of Wednesday through Saturday. That feels great."

Filling the theatre for that longer season will require more public awareness of the Pearl, so I ask Harpster about the effect of the two-column news photo of a scene from *Tartuffe* that appears in today's *New York Times*. By mid-morning there were a dozen telephone calls, plus four calls on the recording machine from Saturday-night readers. Since so many *Times* readers are out of town, the impact of the photo won't be felt immediately, she says, but it is certain that the *Times* reaches more potential customers than any other publication. It is a sad fact that for those interested in addressing serious theatregoers, the *Times* is just about the only game in town.

The sound accompaniment and lighting of *Tartuffe* are being installed today. Looking up from mid-theatre, I see the small,

Members of the cast of Molière's Tartuffe, the season's first play, bowing to each other in the style of seventeenth-century Paris. To teach the actors that style, so essential to playing Molière, Sobel engaged the mime director and teacher Richard Morse, seen above in his one-man show Molière, which was playing at the Pearl while Tartuffe was in rehearsal.

The story of Molière's dark satire centers on Orgon (above left) and the religious con man Tartuffe. Orgon is played by Frank Geraci, and Tartuffe by Martin LaPlatney. Tartuffe sets out to seduce Orgon's wife, Elmire, played by Joanne Camp. The story culminates in the famous table scene, when Tartuffe tries to consummate his seduction of Elmire while her husband is hiding under the table.

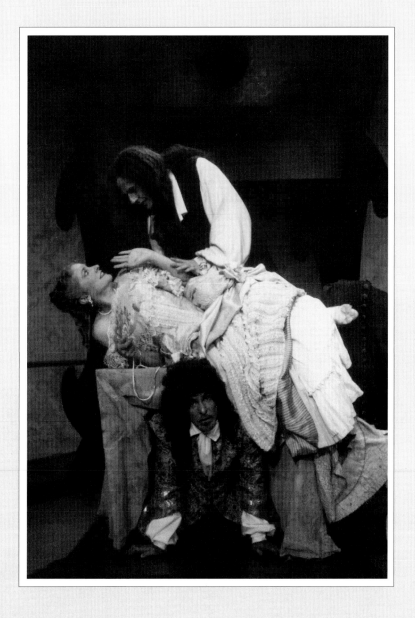

Dorine, the comic and quick-witted maid, is played by Julia Glander (above). Below, Orgon's daughter Mariane, played by Kathryn Lee, vows to crawl to a nunnery rather than obey her father's order to marry the con man Tartuffe. At left is Cléante, Elmire's brother, played by Dugg Smith, a former member of the Pearl company.

jeans-clad figure of Donna Riley on the "balcony," a walkway above and behind the stage that is reached from the second-floor offices. She is installing two large speakers that will pour the music she has chosen into the theatre. Later she will put up two smaller speakers in the lobby.

Richard Kendrick is working at two jobs here, in apparent defiance of his own blue T-shirt that proclaims NOT MY SHOW. He is a tall, rangy man with a look and a twang that accurately suggest he's from somewhere west of the Hudson River. He is the technical director of the theatre at Lafayette College in Easton, Pennsylvania, and he also builds the Pearl's sets, which he brings to New York in sections in his van. Right now he's putting up a wooden bar across the top of the *Tartuffe* set. Sobel requested the bar as a means to make the home pictured in the set "less grandiose" by interrupting the upward sweep of its walls. Sobel is somewhat dissatisfied with the set conceived by his resident designer, Robert Joel Schwartz. "It's too generic seventeenth century," he tells me. "It's not an individual's home. It doesn't scream 'NICE BOURGEOIS HOME IN PARIS.' "

Once the bar is in place, Kendrick moves his ladder to the center of the stage and turns his attention to his other job—as lighting designer for *Tartuffe*. Between trips up the ladder Kendrick explains what he is doing. On some of his trips he is repositioning the lights that shine down from the ceiling on the stage twenty feet below; the lights had been arranged for their own use by the Pearl's two summer tenants. On other trips aloft he is adding color or patterns to the lights. The lights themselves are all white: color or a design can be added by putting a sheet of plastic gel over the bulb.

11:00: The actors are on the stage waiting to rehearse when Sobel announces the startling news that stage manager David Waggett has left. Standing in the aisle, Sobel says: "We have a new stage manager." He points to the big desk in the third row. Behind it we now see the small figure of Lynn Bogarde. She is a short, quiet redhead, whose decade in Australia has left a Commonwealth overlay on her American speech. Bogarde is already known to all of us as the properties mistress notable for her ability to improvise swords and brooms and purses from whatever she can find in or out of the trash. She is a theatre techie who has worked the Pearl's box office when she wasn't doing props or sitting behind the stage manager's desk. Her soft-spoken manner suggests that she will be a very different kind of manager from her forceful, macho predecessor.

David Waggett is leaving under the escape clause in the Equity rules that permits members to break a contract in order to take a better-paying job. (Stage managers are also members of Actors' Equity.) He is leaving for a job at the Goodspeed Opera House in Connecticut. Waggett says Goodspeed pays better than the Pearl's $200 a week and the job will last longer than the remaining seven weeks of *Tartuffe:* stage managers, like actors, are hired for the run of the show.

"Long live the stage manager," Sobel says after he has introduced Bogarde, and the actors give her a round of applause. Sobel is far from unhappy about the change. It is evident from my talks with them that he and Waggett differed on how the rehearsal time should be managed. As I spoke with them I was reminded of Sobel's observation that he has trouble with other males in their forties: a category that includes David Waggett as well as Martin LaPlatney.

As I see them, Sobel and Waggett are two professionals who respect, even admire, each other's abilities, but who have profoundly different attitudes about authority. It is, ultimately, a version of the age-old debate between democracy and dictatorship. Waggett was "very efficient at his job," Sobel said. "But he was too harsh with the actors. If an actor missed a cue, David would reprimand him when he should have asked: 'Can we help?' David acts like a boss, and in art there's no room for a boss. We're all collaborators." That is Sobel's credo as a director, and it also produces the most common criticism of his directing style. Waggett said of that style: "Shep pays too much attention to analysis. He waits for the actor to try it every which way, so the actors aren't sure what he wants, especially those who aren't from the Pearl. It hurts their performance." Waggett found an explanation in Sobel's background as a teacher: "Shep's an educator where he needs to be a coach trying to win the game. He sees the company as a place for training. He gives them parts that are hard for them, to help their growth. But that doesn't make for the best performance if the part is beyond the actor." Waggett praised another result of that concern for the actors: the unusually high proportion of the Pearl's budget that Sobel devotes to their salaries.

After a break, the actors get ready for another run-through. Sobel tells them: "The nature of this rehearsal is for you to test things I don't need to comment on." After the run-through he says the story is less clear but that it has more color. To find out if any of the tempo gained in recent days by his speed-up efforts has been lost, he asks the stage manager for the time: it is one of the stage manager's many responsibilities to time each performance. "An hour fifty-five today, an hour fifty-two yesterday," Lynn Bogarde, our new stage manager, answers. The show is slower by three minutes: some of the tempo has indeed been lost.

Sobel talks to the actors briefly about the coming days that lead up to an opening night now only eleven days away: "Tuesday belongs to the technicians." (That is the day the sound and lighting designers will test their work in the technical rehearsal.) "By Wednesday the show will belong to you." He reminds the actors that they can invite guests to the Thursday dress rehearsal, and concludes: "By Thursday you'll be very ready for an audience."

SEPTEMBER 2

"Costumes give the audience their first impression of the actor. Before the actor speaks a word, the audience sees what he's wearing." That's Barbara Bell, the Pearl's costume designer, on the importance of her work to the actors. We're sitting on the familiar creaky metal chairs in the Pearl's backyard on a sunny day. It's our lunch hour; Bell is spooning from a plastic container mouthfuls of rather tired-looking pasta that she's reheated in the Pearl's microwave. It's from a batch made "by my Italian husband" five days earlier at their upstate home in Cornwall, two hours by bus from the city. During these last days before the show opens, when Bell is spending twelve hours a day at the Pearl, she is sleeping on a couch in a friend's city apartment and living on her husband's pasta. Designers live as close to poverty as actors.

I first met Barbara Bell last spring as a strong, self-confident voice coming over a speakerphone in a production meeting. In person, I find a slender, erect woman in her mid-thirties whose hazel eyes look at you directly through big, clear-rimmed glasses. Her pulled-back hair and the bone structure of her face give her an aristocratic look. Her voice and manner are as direct as her gaze. She answers my questions in straightforward sentences whose intention is never in doubt.

I've already glimpsed the importance of costume in defining the actor in the role. In costume all the actors are different people, and two of them especially are transformed from their contemporary American identities. The Julia Glander whom I've known as a blond roller-blader in biking shorts has vanished under the voluminous skirt and black wig of the maid, Dorine. Martin LaPlatney's long cloak and the straggly, dirty-looking hair of his wig have moved him a long way from the American karate master to the reptilian fraud, Tartuffe.

"I'm known as an actor's designer," Bell says. "I'll work with the actor to make sure anything I put on him is in character. I listen to the actors, to their moods, their emotions, so I don't go in a different direction with their costumes. If an actor's not comfortable in costume, he can't give a good performance. Every detail matters. The last button, the last handbag, the last handkerchief, all the little details are extremely important. If you've got everything right, and then you give him the wrong hat or the wrong jewelry, you've gone against his character. That can spoil his performance because the actor will notice it even if the audience doesn't. You might not see those details on a large stage with three thousand seats, but this is a small house and all the details show. I like that. Another big plus at the Pearl is the resident company. I know these bodies very well. I know what works on them and what doesn't. I've worked through all the little trouble spots. I know you can't cut this one off at this level because it just makes him look shorter than ever. I know this one has a skinny neck and not much shoulder, so this look is not good for him." She's willing to compromise authenticity for the actors' sake. She put an extra lift in Frank Geraci's shoes to bring him closer to the three six-footers in the cast, and when LaPlatney told her he had to be able to pull his pants down easily (in the table scene with Elmire), she agreed to put elastic in them, although elastic was unknown to the seventeenth century.

The Pearl's minuses have mostly to do with lack of money. This is the first season she will design all five shows. Because the Pearl successfully applied for a grant from the Princess Grace Foundation for costume design, Bell will get twice the pay per show she got last year. The Pearl budget provides $5,500 for designing and making costumes for the entire season, leaving it to Bell to apportion the spending among the five shows. Like everyone at the Pearl, she is adept at stretching her dollars. She cannibalizes what she can from the Pearl's collection, which lines the walls of her second-floor space; but she hasn't been able to use much from the Pearl's production of Molière's *The School for Wives* because fashions changed too much in the ten years between the writing of the two plays. She rented some of the *Tartuffe* costumes from the Costume Collection on Twenty-sixth Street, and some from the Milwaukee Rep and the Rutgers University theatre. Under the terms of these rentals, Bell is allowed to make alterations as long as all the material is returned intact.

But she still has to "build" the costumes as well as design them: "I'm a seamstress and a designer." Since she's paid only as a designer, Bell calculates that she donates half to three-quarters of the time she spends working at the Pearl—or for the Pearl, since she does much of her work in the basement of her home upstate. "If I'm doing a big build show I can get fourteen hours of uninterrupted work in my basement," she says. She performs her seamstress duties at some cost to her health. She is often laid low with back trouble, and she has to wear an arm support when she works at her sewing machine. "It wrecks my arm and it makes me crabby," she says of her work at the machine. "Most of all, it doesn't allow me to be a designer. Everything is last-minute."

I ask how she got into design. "I'm definitely a costume person who happened to go into theatre," she says. This is in contrast to Donna Riley, who a few days earlier told me she was "a theatre person who went into sound design." Bell had originally wanted to design costumes for film because "in film you notice everything, all the intricate little things. That's what I love." She went into theatre design because more schools offered training in it. Like most people around the Pearl, she's from somewhere outside New York. Bell was born in Valparaiso, Indiana, and got her training at Florida Atlantic University and Rutgers. After eight years working in regional theatre in Miami and Houston, she and the man to whom she is now married—a backstage theatre person who is now a general contractor—decided it was time to "move East and hit New York." They settled in Cornwall because it was rural, which they wanted, but accessible to work for both of them. She estimates she's designed more than a hundred shows. When I ask her to name a favorite, she pauses uncharacteristically, then recalls a "splendid black *Oedipus*" set in Egypt. She says she never repeats her designs: "I've done *Glass Menagerie* three times, and each time it was different."

I ask about alternatives to her present difficult life. "I constantly think about chucking this for better pay and an easier life," she says. "This design job never gets glamorous—those days are gone. It isn't going to get any easier. My husband says he's going to take me away from all this." She shakes her head. "It's a heavy question in my mind. But what am I going to do? I'd like to design for film, but that means starting at the bottom. I don't want to do fashion. What I really want is for the Pearl to get a real costume shop so I can stop being a seamstress and be a designer."

With that, Bell excuses herself to spray-paint some shoes, a task she does a few feet away from the table where we've been sitting. She is spraying Damis's shoes with a basic coat of dark blue followed by a sprinkling of white. While she sprays, Bell explains what she is doing in her usual short, declarative sentences: "A single coat is flat. I hate a flat look. Mixing colors gives texture. I like texture."

SEPTEMBER 3

9:30: This is tech day. In the morning the sound and light designers will go over their work with the director and stage manager, and with the two apprentices who will operate the equipment. First comes "dry tech"—dry because it's done without actors. This afternoon we'll rehearse sound and light with the cast.

The lighting designer, Richard Kendrick, is up in the booth with Colleen Davis, the young apprentice stage manager who will operate the lights. At the Pearl, the booth is truly up—you get there by climbing a ladder from the lobby. It's a long, narrow passageway above the last row of the theatre. The stage manager will "call" the show, giving their cues by intercom to the sound and light operators, from a tiny desk in the booth. The lights operator sits near the stage manager and has three kinds of lights to run. The house lights, those that illuminate the theatre when the show is not playing, are raised and dimmed by turning a heavy wheel that looks as if it belongs on a pipeline valve. The work lights over the stage are used only for rehearsal. The show lights are those that light the stage during performance. These number thirty for *Tartuffe* and are controlled from a board with two banks of twenty-four rheostats that raise and dim the lights. Although they are only about three feet apart in the booth, the stage manager will give her cues—sixty-one for *Tartuffe*—to the lights operator over her intercom: the booth is only a few feet over the heads of the audience, so the stage manager cannot speak in much more than a whisper.

Backstage, Donna Riley is looking over the sound controls. The sound for *Tartuffe* will be operated by Janine Lindsay, the tall young British apprentice who is in her second season at the Pearl (and who has a nonspeaking role in *Tartuffe* as Flipote, Madame Pernelle's maid). The sound system holds up to four tapes that can be played in any combination or mixture over the two speakers above the stage and the smaller second pair in the lobby. The apprentice running the sound operates the sound board on cues she receives over her headset from the stage manager up in the booth. For *Tartuffe*, there are thirty cues. All are for music: Donna Riley plans no sound effects in this show.

Now the operators take their places and the two designers join Sobel and Lynn Bogarde behind the big homemade desk in one of the middle rows. Bogarde calls the cues and everyone watches the lighting and listens to the sound. The lighting changes seem to me to be very subtle, and Sobel says to Kendrick: "You can go ahead and be more obvious. Subliminal messages are irrelevant. We're playing it pretty out front." Kendrick, who is following the cues in his script, occasionally explains where we are:

"This is when Dorine is signaling Mariane behind Orgon's back" (the light shifts slightly to Dorine) or "This highlights Valère's shtik." In general, Kendrick tells me, he uses a warm pink light for the women, a "cold, unhealthy" light for the villain, Tartuffe. For the big scene between Orgon and his daughter, Mariane, he provides a "bleeding-heart special." Kendrick can't do everything he would like. About Tartuffe's first entrance, he says: "I'd have liked a special light for the door, but I thought lighting Tartuffe was more important and I ran out of instruments." When they do the first scene between Tartuffe and Elmire, Lynn Bogarde scrambles up on stage to mark with bits of tape where the two chairs should be placed to catch the light. "Does everyone agree with me that that streak has to go?" Sobel asks.

Sobel wants to add music to some of the lines. "Let's try it," he suggests. "We'll know if it's right when we hear it." To Donna Riley he says: "For Orgon's last speech, music under the speech, triumphant and even a little bit romantic." Riley nods.

During a break the four people gathered at Lynn Bogarde's desk swap theatre stories. One is about the fresh-faced young actress appearing for an audition whose first words were: "Who do I have to fuck around here to get hired?"

At the lunch hour I ask Sobel whether he's pleased with the sound and light. "We're as happy as we can get in dry tech," he answers. I observe that he seems less than joyful today. "This is the worst week for my kind of director," he says. I know by now he means a director who does not simply walk away from the show when his contractual obligation is finished. "This is when I have to disengage and give the show to Lynn and the actors. I should get out of town." He smiles a bit sheepishly, as if to acknowledge that we both know he won't be anyplace but here.

The doorbell rings, and I am deputized to answer. It's a process server. I look around uncertainly, but Mary Harpster appears as if on cue and quietly takes the problem off everyone's hands but her own.

1:30: The actors are here, and it's time for a cue-to-cue tech rehearsal. The veteran actress Anna Minot comes on stage while we're waiting to begin. "I like the footlights. They're flattering," she says. Dorine, out of her corset and back in biking shorts, makes a game of scratching herself with the period broom Lynn Bogarde made for her when she was still props mistress.

Bogarde, now as stage manager, asks the actors to give just the lines that precede sound and light cues. The lights lose Dorine in the first scene. Several scenes later Sobel says to Kendrick: "Cléante has fallen out of the light. Do you have any more to give him?"

During a ten-minute break Arnie Burton and Kathryn Lee go out in the backyard to work on a single moment: when Mariane and Valère take each other's hand, at Dorine's instruction, and exchange a glance. It is a very delicate moment. As in much of the play, and much of Molière, the mood of that glance is balanced on a fine edge between the comic and the poignant. We can laugh at the lovers' foolishness, or we can feel a pang of sympathy for their torment; and if Burton and Lee get it just right, we'll do both at once.

❧ SEPTEMBER 8

1:45: The little lobby is crowded with people. Shep Sobel is moving among them, gracefully fielding questions about *Tartuffe* and the Pearl. He is doing what he would like someone to do before every performance: schmoozing with the audience. Lively seventeenth-century music is playing over the lobby's two speakers. The music is putting people in the mood: I see a white-haired woman jigging to its rapid beat.

Today's preview performance is almost sold out. That's because the Pearl offers subscribers a lower rate for these early shows before audiences are attracted by reviews or word of mouth. We're going to see the fourth of six previews. This is the first year the Pearl has given previews; in previous years the Pearl, like other Off Off Broadway houses, went straight from dress rehearsal to opening night. Time was when shows headed for Broadway played out of town first to test their work in front of an audience before they faced the New York reviewers. Today the preview serves the same function, but now the only difference between this performance and the regular run of the play is that the reviewers are asked not to come before opening night.

Today's ushers are Donna Riley, the sound designer whose music selections we're hearing, and Diane Paulus, an understudy. It's also the Pearl's first season for understudies. In the past the Pearl took its chances, and if an actor was unable to go on the show closed for that performance. But the new Equity contract requires understudies. For *Tartuffe* there are four, two of whom are the two non-Equity actors in the cast. The two outside understudies are paid $200 to stand by for the seven weeks of the run, and they earn credits toward Equity membership. They must be off book—that is, know their lines—before the show opens, and they must appear for three or four rehearsals with the stage manager at which they learn the blocking. They must call the theatre forty-five minutes to an hour before each show and leave a number at which they can be reached. The understudies in the cast get no extra pay.

The house lights dim, stage lights go up, Madame Pernelle storms on stage—the show is on. As I watch Molière's familiar story unfold, I marvel at the distance the show has traveled since that morning four weeks and five days ago when the actors gathered around the table on this stage to read the script to each other. In the interim they've made of that script their own unique *Tartuffe*, different from any other *Tartuffe* ever played, different also from the hundred versions that briefly lived and died during rehearsal. With the costumes and the set, and the lights and the music, they've moved themselves from the twentieth to the seventeenth century. And, we in the orchestra hope, they will move us with them. I am aware as never before of the difference it makes for the actors to play not to their familiar ground crew but to seventy-odd strangers who sit out here, expectant, waiting for the actors to tell us who they are, to feed our eyes and ears, our hearts and minds, waiting for Molière and the actors to take us to a time and place we've never been and tell us a tale we've never heard about people we've never met.

Today's show goes well. The audience is attentive and appreciative. As far as I can tell, they're enjoying the show. Often people chuckle instead of laughing so as not to miss the next line. They love the two scenes between Tartuffe and Elmire that were so troublesome in rehearsal; the table scene draws applause as well as laughter. Dorine's several comic moments are well received. At the close—there's no curtain at the Pearl—the applause is hearty if not deafening.

I notice several minor bobbles. When, in the first scene, Dorine snaps an imaginary fan, one of the other women is supposed to snap a real fan; today that real snap is missing, and what the audience hears is the sound of no fan snapping. Cléante loses a couple of lines. Elmire's dress snags momentarily on the table during that big scene. There's also a peculiar moment in the scene in which Damis, played by young Hank Wagner, emerges from the closet to interrupt the first encounter between Elmire and Tartuffe with "No, Madame . . ." I notice Joanne Camp as Elmire stop in a strange pause, then resume for a couple of lines before Wagner emerges.

I learn what happened when, half an hour after the show, Wagner meets Camp on the empty stage. I hear him say in a pleading tone, arms spread wide: "I'm sorry, I'm sorry, I'm sorry!" Camp is not mollified. She says to him slowly in a voice harsh with anger: "You—left—two people—stranded on stage. It took me a long time to get back into the scene." Hank Wagner missed his cue to come out of the closet: that much I understand. But, I ask Camp, why that pause just before the end of her speech? She smiles and says: "I know Hank, so I was prepared in case he missed his cue. Those last two lines were mine." This

extraordinarily conscientious performer had composed a couplet
for just such an emergency. Molière plus Camp goes like this:
Molière:

ELMIRE: Give up your own inequitable plan
To take a girl pledged to another man
And . . .

(Here Damis is supposed to interrupt her with "No, Madame . . .")
Camp's couplet reads:

And . . . restore harmony to the family
Who has offered you such warm company

Late that afternoon, when the sun is about to set, I am talking
with Camp in the backyard. She has shed Elmire's corset and
multiple skirts and wig, and is sitting comfortably in jeans with
her strawberry-blond hair around her shoulders. We're talking
about Elmire for the second time. A month earlier, on the eve of
rehearsal, Camp told me about her preparation for the role of
Orgon's wife. She'd already spent three or four hours a day over
a span of four weeks preparing for *Tartuffe.* "I've been reading the
play over and over. Some actors study the period, but I spend
more time on the text," she'd said then. "There's a danger if you
concentrate on the period that you'll play the period instead of
your character. I look for differences between my character and
myself. One big difference is that Elmire has more confidence in
herself than I do. She has a better sense of humor, she has
compassion for human frailty. It comes out in how well she
handles her first scene with Tartuffe. She stays calm where I'd
have been totally unreasonable. That's a good difference to
know about. It helps me not get too upset about things in my
own life, like what men say to me on the street.

"I've surprised myself about Elmire," she says now. "The
challenge in playing Elmire is that she's seldom doing what she

says she's doing. Anna helped me out when I was having a terrible time with my first scene with Orgon. [Anna Minot is the veteran actress who is playing Madame Pernelle.] This is where I respond after Orgon says he doesn't believe what we're telling him about Tartuffe. I couldn't get it right, so I asked Anna to listen on the monitor. [What's happening on stage is transmitted to speakers in the dressing rooms so the actors can hear their cues.] Afterwards Anna said to me: 'What you're really saying here is, Don't call me a liar. I'm telling you the truth!' That gave me what I needed to know. The audience helps me too. In the table scene I've been having trouble keeping Frank in mind. [Frank Geraci, playing Orgon, is hidden under the table.] But the audience knows he's there, and that helps me stay aware of him."

I ask about the effect of the daily vocal exercises she conducts. "You can't make it all happen in half an hour a day," she says. "Still, it's helped us be aware of our vocal problems and our breathing needs. Our pronunciation differences are only minor now. Julia [Glander] and Kathryn [Lee] are excited about the vocal work and of course that's endeared them to me. I think it's been particularly important to Julia. She had a severe nasality problem—her voice would go nasal on her at times. It reminds me of the voice problem I had when I was younger. But now she's more comfortable vocally and her voice opens up nicely." Camp goes on to say that she's happy with this company, of whom several members are new to her. "It's been more fun than I thought it would be. No one is lazy this year," she says. "We get along well. In some productions of *Tartuffe,* there's a lot of rivalry, especially between Elmire and Dorine. But Julia and I depend on each other, and she and I and Kathryn can all be totally silly in the dressing room."

With opening night three performances away, what remains to be done? "My first scene with Tartuffe isn't quite right yet," Camp says. "I want to work more on style, make my crosses more interesting. I'd like more choreography in act five." She turns then to a problem that haunts anyone playing Molière, this

writer in whom the comic and the tragic are so closely inter-
woven. "There's a troubling question about this play," she says.
"It can be quite dark. How dark is it supposed to get?"

❧ SEPTEMBER II

Rehearsals continue on a reduced schedule—three hours a day
instead of six—during this week of previews leading up to tomorrow night's gala opening.

We're wrestling with "Poor fellow!"—the scene that once
seemed difficult and now seems impossible—and it's obvious
that Sobel and Frank Geraci are still dissatisfied with each other
as well as with the scene.

Everyone is looking at the scene in the light of the audience's
response during previews. "They're not getting it," Julia
Glander says unhappily, and she takes the blame: "I'm not
setting it up for them." "One time it worked," offers Dugg
Smith, whose Cléante is a silent presence during the scene. But
then he adds: "Whatever *it* was."

Sobel suggests a new position to Glander, whose Dorine has
the difficult task of communicating with Cléante while ostensibly
speaking only to her master, Orgon. Glander's mood suddenly
brightens when she finds a move that draws a laugh, at least here
in rehearsal. "That's it! I know it'll work!" she exclaims, and,
always eager to translate thoughts into movement, she jumps in
the air and clicks her heels.

Despite such good moments, no one really believes the scene
has been repaired for tomorrow night's opening. "I'm lost,"
Sobel confesses at one point.

When I talk with Sobel after rehearsal, I find that his misgiv-
ings go far beyond the "Poor fellow!" scene. He is troubled by
the work of the same two actors with whom he's been at odds

since the early rehearsals, the actors who play the two central roles—Martin LaPlatney's Tartuffe and Frank Geraci's Orgon. "I'm keeping their wounds open," he says. "I'm asking them to change their performances."

Of LaPlatney he says: "I won't get the performance from Martin I'd hoped for. He's not tuned in to what I'm telling him about language. He responded with scorn to the note he got on diction from Robert." Robert Neff Williams, the Pearl's voice coach, made written comments to some of the actors after attending a preview.

Sobel's criticism of the Pearl veteran Frank Geraci is more basic: "Frank's not taking his responsibility for the play. Orgon is the quarterback, and the actor playing him has to drive the play, but Frank doesn't want to do that. That keeps surfacing no matter what I say to him." Sobel also finds in Geraci's performance a common failing that theatre people call "playing the character's attorney"; the actor wants the audience to sympathize with the character he is playing. Sobel cites the scene in which Orgon tells his daughter, Mariane, that she has to marry Tartuffe. Orgon is momentarily touched by her pleas, but she is unable to deflect him from his decision. "Instead of playing the action, Frank is trying to explain Orgon to the audience," Sobel tells me. "He's trying to show us Orgon's pain and struggle. He's saying he's doing it to her for her own good. But Orgon didn't explain. He just did it because he was driven to it. Of course an actor needs to know the why, why his character does what he does. But he shouldn't *play* the why. After all, the character isn't thinking about the why. He's just doing it."

Geraci, when I spoke with him a couple of days earlier, was "upset" with Sobel's criticism, but he also had some complaints to make about Sobel's directing. "I went home after Shep gave me his notes. I refused to blame myself. I know there's something right about what I'm doing. I went over the script, I tried to combine what Shep wants and what I want. He told me to watch out for going falsetto. Falsetto means I've lost control, it's not coming from the pelvis, and that's because I'm not fully grounded in my character. When I'm sure of my character, I feel an inner quietness, and the character comes out in my eyes. Otherwise I'm likely to go to grimaces, vaudeville turns, tricks I've learned." He saw the scene with Mariane differently from Sobel. "The key is my absolute certainty that I know what's right for her and for my family. I'm saying to Mariane, 'I'm your father, I *know* what's good for you.' "

Geraci blamed what he saw as Sobel's negative style of directing. "I keep saying to him, 'Don't tell me what not to do, tell me what you want,' " he said. "Shep and I haven't gotten along. He's no help in physical staging. We actors have to save each other. For him, radio theatre would be great. I know I give him a hard time, but Shep shouldn't direct on stage. Of course, you're hearing this from an actor who wants to direct." He shrugged. "This culminates eight years at the Pearl!"

He recalled as a "wonderful accident" finding an account of Stanislavski directing *Tartuffe* that included an interpretation of Orgon's religious belief as it affected his behavior in the "Poor fellow!" scene and the next scene with Cléante. "I felt as if Stanislavski were teaching a class and he'd given me a note about Orgon. I wanted to say: 'Holy shit, thank you, Stanislavski!' "

Several days earlier Sobel had considered letting the show stand as it was. "I'd decided to disengage and say, 'This is the best show I can get with these actors.' But then I thought, That's the wrong response. I'll try again to get the best show I can. A lot rides on this production. Whether people like it enough to subscribe for next year. Whether we get substantial grants from foundations. Whether the board approves the leap we're taking." He shook his head. "I can still tinker with it, but right now it's not a good show."

Tonight's gala opening of *Tartuffe* is the first big social event of the Pearl's season. It's partly a fund-raiser: tickets go for seventy-five dollars rather than the usual twelve to sixteen dollars. Mostly, though, it's a rare opportunity for the two branches of the Pearl family—those who raise the money and those who put on the shows—to eat and drink and party together, after the show, which tonight will start at seven o'clock. Everyone is dressed up. Board members tend toward the formal, actors toward party costumes. Sobel, whom I've only seen in a necktie once or twice, is resplendent in a tuxedo, which he wears with his usual grace.

When I arrive at 5:30 the caterers are busy setting up equipment in the backyard; fortunately there's no hint of rain. When I pass the bulletin board on the way to the back door I notice an envelope inviting people to give to the struggle against AIDS as an alternative to the traditional opening-night gift. While I'm watching the caterers deploy their wares, Sobel appears and says he would like "a private word" with me. He walks me out of earshot and says quietly: "We've just learned that Ivan has AIDS-related pneumonia. He won't be back here. I didn't want you to hear it by rumor." Ivan Polley is the Pearl's fund-raiser who's been out, supposedly with the flu, since mid-August. I ask about the impact of the news on the Pearl family. "Something like this is bound to set off a wave of fear among those who are at risk," Sobel says. "Even those who haven't tested positive." I'm not surprised, given the well-known prevalence of AIDS in the world of the theatre. Sobel goes back in the theatre, leaving me to reflect about the very personable, quiet young man I'd only begun to know, and whom I am now quite sure I will not see again; and I think also about the man who would take the trouble, on one of the most important evenings of his life, to make sure I get the story straight.

In the lobby Robin Leslie Brown, a small, dark-haired member of the Pearl company, is greeting the cast with *"Merde!,"* the French equivalent of the American actors' good-luck wish "Break a leg!" A tall, thin Pearl actor, Stuart Lerch, is holding a bunch of balloons. In the theatre I notice two seats reserved for "Jones," which Sobel tells me are for reviewers. For fear that if the actors know critics are present it might affect a performance, Mary Harpster disguises their seats under assumed names, which she regularly changes. There isn't, in any event, the suspense about reviews that attends an opening night on Broadway: no one is going to wait up for the early editions. The reviews will dribble out over the coming weeks, and are relatively unimportant to attendance at the Pearl.

The show goes smoothly, with only a few minor bobbles, and afterwards the staff and volunteers set up tables of food and drink on the stage. A festive crowd gathers as soon as the cast is out of costume. We mill around sampling chicken crepes and ratatouille and sipping jug wine. Most of the trustees are about the same age as most of the actors and they all seem to be mingling easily. I find myself with Ken Rotman, the president of the trustees, and his wife, Kate. Rotman is telling a story about Sobel's fabled austerity. According to Rotman, a couple of years ago, when the trustees told Sobel they were going to raise his annual salary of $8,000, he threatened to quit unless they retracted the raise. Rotman contrasts this with the artistic director of another Off Broadway company, not much bigger than the Pearl, who Rotman said told him he was raising his own salary to $34,000 "because he was marrying a Russian ballerina." I have to remind myself that both salaries are microscopic by the standards of the business world.

Later on I have an opportunity to ask Sobel how he views his work after the opening and eight preview performances. "The audiences are enjoying it," he acknowledges, and what he says next reminds me of the extraordinary standard by which he measures the Pearl: "But I don't think we've changed anybody's life, which is what I'd like to do. We've gotten a level or two under their skin, but we haven't gotten down to where we want to get. Molière did his job, we haven't done ours." I observe that the audience one night laughed at Mariane's big emotional scene when she tells her father she'll go to a nunnery if he makes her marry Tartuffe, while on another night they seemed closer to tears. "Which way the audience responds depends on very subtle differences in what Kathryn [Lee] and the others do," he tells me. Which response does he seek? "Both. It should be funny to the point of ridiculous when she collapses into 'let me drag my sad steps' and there she is walking on her knees. It's ridiculous but it's true. We have to believe that she really means what she's saying, that she's in great adolescent pain. Adolescent pain is the worst pain we ever feel and it can be very funny to everyone else. So we want the audience laughing through their tears, or crying through their giggles."

When I ask if he expects the show to change, Sobel says he hopes the actors will grow in their roles, and goes on to draw a fine line: "The difference between growing in the role and changing is very delicate. On the one hand, you don't want to suddenly do something the other actors can't respond to. But if you do exactly the same thing every night, that would be movies, not theatre. When you go out on stage, there's an enormous amount you have to do to present the character we developed in rehearsal, *and* there's an enormous amount you must do to keep it fresh and first-time, to keep the freedom to play with it. Finding the balance between the two is why it's art."

Sobel telephones me at home at around nine o'clock. It's the first day of rehearsal for *The Trojan Women*, but that isn't what's on his mind.

"This is one of those terrible phone calls," Sobel says. "Ivan is gone." The end came very fast for Ivan Polley, the Pearl's director of development. He was still at work in mid-August. Two weeks ago we were told he had AIDS-related pneumonia. Now he is dead at thirty-four.

In the Pearl's lobby an hour later I find Joanne Camp and Arnie Burton hugging and crying and talking about Ivan Polley. Burton says in a wondering tone: "So many friends . . ." Young men stricken down at random by a malignant fate: it begins to feel like the war years of long ago.

Half a dozen of us are in the theatre, waiting for rehearsal, when Sobel returns from taking a telephone call. Standing in the aisle, he tells us that the call was about Ivan. In his last days Ivan had asked that his body be cremated and the ashes divided between his two worlds: the rural Kentucky of his upbringing and the New York of his profession. But, according to Sobel, cremation was against his parents' religious beliefs. "He couldn't even have that," Sobel says, and then for the first time since I've known him he loses his self-possession. A sob rises in his throat and tears fill his eyes. Joanne Camp hurries up the aisle and embraces her husband. Hank Wagner, the apprentice actor who's been around the Pearl since he was in high school, comes up and awkwardly embraces Camp and Sobel from behind. For a very long moment the three of them stand locked together like a sculptured monument to grief.

Now there appears in the doorway a figure from another,

ancient world of sorrow—the great tragic heroine Hecuba, in the person of Bella Jarrett, the veteran actress who will portray her. Sobel pulls himself together with a visible effort. "You really walked in on something," he says to Bella Jarrett. He shakes his head as if to clear it of other thoughts and says firmly: "Let's rehearse."

Once again we are seated on stage around the improvised table to hear the actors read the play. *The Trojan Women* takes place outside the walls of Troy just after the city has fallen to the Greeks. The widows and daughters of Troy's leaders are gathered to hear their fate: they are told each in turn by a Greek envoy that they will be parceled out as slaves to the victorious Greek chieftains. Hecuba, widow of Troy's King Priam and the central figure in the play, has been given to Odysseus, whom the Trojans consider the most evil of the Greeks. Her daughter-in-law Andromache, Hector's widow, must watch as the Greeks take away and kill her young son. In contrast to all the other women, Cassandra, the virgin priestess raped by the Greeks, comes on stage laughing, because she can see the future, so she knows the victors' fate will be even worse than what they are doing to the Trojans. Late in the play, King Menelaus of Sparta comes to reclaim the cause of the war, his wife, Helen, but doesn't know what to do with her. The play ends with Hecuba, who has been on stage throughout, hobbling painfully off— "Forward:/into the slave's life."

As the actors read, I am astonished by how clearly Euripides speaks to me across the gap of twenty-four centuries. That many of the names and references are unknown to me makes little difference. Athenian audiences of the fifth century B.C. knew the myths the story draws on better than we do, and were accustomed, as we are not, to its dramatic methods, yet it is hard to imagine that they could have been more moved by it than we are today. Can anyone shed more tears than these?

After the reading Sobel talks to us about the play's meaning. He notes that Euripides was writing about what was already the remote past, a time more of myth than of history. It's generally believed that he wrote not to denounce the distant misdeeds of the Greek conquerors of Troy, but in horrified response to war crimes committed in his time by his fellow Athenians—and today we can similarly see the play as a commentary on our own bloodstained century. The Hecuba of Euripides finds that message to future generations in her people's fate:

> The gods meant nothing except to make life hard for me,
> and of all cities they chose Troy to hate. In vain
> we sacrificed. And yet had not the very hand
> of God gripped and crushed this city deep in the ground,
> we should have disappeared in darkness, and not given
> a theme for music, and the songs of men to come.

Sobel pauses after reading Hecuba's lines. "That's why Hecuba goes on instead of killing herself, for the songs of men to come," he says. "That's what Euripides wants us to remember." And he adds: "And that's why I do theatre."

Some inner voice evidently warns him that his last statement may sound a bit pretentious to this audience, so he smiles and says, to an appreciative laugh: "Well—that, and the money!"

Donnah Welby would have been the first to mock any pretension on Sobel's part. Welby, who will play Andromache, has been a member of the Pearl's resident acting company since its earliest days. She is beautiful in the full-faced, dark-haired manner of Elizabeth Taylor in her thirties. She is the most private member of the company, and the most playful. When I asked her the year of her birth, she parried me with: "Cut off my arm and count the rings!" Then she exploded into laughter.

We were sitting in a low-cost restaurant near her Times Square office. Alone among Pearl actors, Welby has another job that is something better than a way to pay the rent. She is an executive at the Theatre Development Fund, which gave her two months' leave for *The Trojan Women*.

I discovered Welby's privacy when she was describing how she summons the emotions she needs. "Each of us has a golden box, as my acting teacher Michael Howard calls it. We have things in that golden box that are very private, things that affect us deeply, events in our lives that we can still cry about. We use them again and again and again in our work to achieve an effect or an impression. Most of us have only a couple of those life experiences that we can use. If you've had a rough life, you might have eight or nine. They're our secrets, what we call on for grief, or love, or hate. We call on them and tailor them for each play or character. We never talk about them." Why must they be secret? I asked. "If they weren't secret they'd lose their magic," Welby said. "If you knew I was crying about something from my childhood rather than about losing my son, it would be a different experience for you. If the whole audience knew it, it'd be a different play."

Why, I wondered, does so private a person choose to turn her emotions inside out in front of a theatre full of strangers? "It's liberating, just because I'm so private," Welby explained. "It's such a risk for me, it's so daring to do anything in front of other people. Some people climb Mount Everest, I go out on a stage. It's a way of revealing myself without losing my privacy. Even if I do reveal a lot about myself, no one will ever know it except me because I'm always out there as someone else."

Welby was willing to talk about some of the ways she summoned the emotions she needed to portray Andromache's loss of her son and her husband. For Hector, Andromache's dead husband, she used the image of a man from whom she'd recently parted: "He's alive, but he's sure dead for me!" Again I heard her marvelously raucous laugh. "I've never lost a son"—Welby has no children—"but I've known death. We actors tend to be pretty emotional people, we overemotionalize everything, so my reaction to losing a dear friend could be similar to a normal person's reaction to losing a child." She said she also uses sense memory to summon her emotions: "The smell of oil of roses reminds me of funeral parlors. I might smell it before going on, or think about smelling it when I'm on stage. That puts me right into a place of death."

Andromache, I observed, seemed a remarkably different woman from the actress who was going to play her. Welby's reply surprised me: "Inside every active, self-determined woman there's a genetic memory of that loyal and obedient wife."

Like other actors here, Welby believes her own life is affected by the character she is portraying. "I'm somewhat apprehensive about living for two months with the circumstances this woman is going through. It can't help but spill over into my day, my life." She recalled going home on the subway one night when she was playing Lady Macbeth in what actors always call "the Scottish Play" (because speaking its name supposedly brings bad luck): "There was this street person playing the saxophone and saying: 'Hi, I'm an alien and I'm trying to raise money to get back to my planet.' He was awful, he couldn't play the sax at all. People were paying him to stop playing. And suddenly there I am standing up and yelling at him: 'If you don't stop I'll throw you off this train!' Luckily he didn't take me up on it. I'd never have done that if I hadn't been coming off playing Lady Macbeth."

Among the many parts she's played in her years at the Pearl is Olga in Chekhov's *Three Sisters*. Welby mentioned that role when I asked why she likes working at the Pearl: "No one else would cast me as Olga. Other theatres are always casting me as a vixen, a bitch, the other woman." Welby's dark beauty and knowing manner made it clear to me why casting directors aren't likely to think of her for innocents like Olga. She enjoys playing the classics because the author gives the actors all they need. She said, paraphrasing Shaw: "You act the lines, the play's all in the lines. You don't have to act between the lines." To illustrate, she began to fuss with her hair while she was talking. When she saw my eyes stray to her hands, meaning she'd succeeded in attracting my attention to the gesture rather than the line, she said with the air of someone who's scored with her rapier: "There, that's what I mean!" Donnah Welby seemed to me to stand somewhat aloof from the Pearl family. She shrugged off a question about that relationship with: "The Pearl belongs to Shep and Joanne. I don't have any say in it."

◟ SEPTEMBER 26

How do gods behave on stage when one god is the other's uncle? The question comes up in the first scene of *The Trojan Women,* which is a conversation between Poseidon and his niece Athene. Besides being deities, and relatives, the two were opponents in the Trojan War. Poseidon is the patron god of Troy, and the Greeks won with the help of Athene.

No one, of course, knows how Euripides conceived his gods nor how they were interpreted in his day. Seeking clues to their nature, the cast turns to the myths and the other plays in which the gods appear, as do several of the mortal characters in the story. Sobel passes out a map of Greece at Euripides' time and a chart showing the pantheon of the gods. Hearing the actors stumble over unfamiliar names, he sends an apprentice looking for a pronouncing dictionary of Greek names.

Looking at the actors portraying the gods—Stuart Lerch's Poseidon wears a baseball cap turned backward; Robin Leslie Brown's Athene sports a Giants sweatshirt a couple of sizes too big for her—leads me to wonder how gods dress as well as behave. I ask the costume designer, Barbara Bell, but the question is premature. "The gods are on hold," she informs me.

Lerch and Brown are Pearl veterans who have played together over and over and who will appear together again in *The Trojan Women* as Menelaus and Helen.

Lerch is a tall, slender man in his late thirties. He was passed over by Sobel for the role of Tartuffe. As he told it, Sobel thought Lerch was "manufacturing" his emotions in his audition and could not convey the "driven" nature of Tartuffe. Lerch took the loss philosophically; he strikes me as outwardly the least emotional member of the company. He seemed to half agree with

Sobel's judgment. "I know I could play a con man," he said, "but I might have trouble thinking from the penis."

Tartuffe is on Sobel's mind today. During a break he tells me Martin LaPlatney has notified him that he is on a short list for the commercial for which he auditioned three weeks ago. If he gets the assignment he'll be away for two or three days. Sobel doesn't know what he'll do if that happens. He doesn't take seriously the understudy arrangement required by the new Equity contract; it might be better to close down for those performances. Sobel is obviously irritated; it doesn't help that the person causing the problem is the actor with whom he had so much trouble in rehearsal. Yet LaPlatney is entirely within his rights. What's left unspoken is that this is bound to happen in a world in which theatres like the Pearl can pay talented actors like LaPlatney only $180 a week. (He didn't get the commercial.)

When I see Lerch and Brown again later in the afternoon, they are Menelaus and Helen. They are seeing each other for the first time since Helen set off the war ten years earlier by running off with the Trojan prince Paris. Menelaus has come to reclaim and perhaps kill his errant wife. There's little to admire about Menelaus; in preparing to play him, Lerch was seeking an animal image, and those that came to his mind were a rat and a hyena. In his first bumbling speech Menelaus makes clear that he doesn't know what to do with Helen now that he has her. That same speech invites us, the audience, to reflect on the trivial cause and futile outcome of a war in which so many have suffered or died.

Helen is cornered and alone in the world. Both the Greeks and the Trojans hate her, and Hecuba pleads with Menelaus to kill her. Her only chance is to win back her husband. Sobel and Brown go over the text in order to master the case she makes to Menelaus that it was she who saved the Greeks from the Trojans. Helen makes several tries at it, and Sobel tells Brown to "save her desperation for the last speech."

Brown has been at the Pearl since its beginning and has known Sobel since he directed her in her first high school performance two decades ago. We spoke one evening after sunset in the Pearl's backyard. She is a very small and well-proportioned woman with abundant, flowing black hair and aquiline features that give her a Mediterranean look. What you are likely to sense in Robin Leslie Brown is her intensity. She puts as much emotional force into our conversation as she does into her work on stage. She has a piercing gaze and a low, resonant voice with an unusual range. She is a voice coach on the side and she often leads the Pearl's preshow vocal warm-up.

Brown loves acting so much she even loves the fear that goes with each performance. "It's as exciting as sex," she said. "You never know how you're going to do." Her voice is particularly intense when she talks about the fictional people who have shared her inner space. She treasures them all, but mostly the ones she enjoyed playing or cared deeply about. "I love being Barbara!" she said of the title role in Shaw's *Major Barbara*. The present tense is intended: Brown keeps Barbara alive for the pleasure of her presence, but Bérénice—of Racine's *Bérénice*—lives on because of Brown's loyalty to the doomed Hebrew queen. She recalled her epic battle with Sobel to salvage some dignity for Bérénice after she has been rejected by the Roman Emperor. "Shep wouldn't leave her even a shred!" she said, blue eyes flashing, as indignant as if the rejection had happened to Brown herself, not to Bérénice, yesterday, not three years ago. In an emotional sense it *had* happened to Brown herself, long ago on a lakeside dock in upstate New York. That's where her father left his young daughter, who longed to go out fishing with him. When she was preparing to go on stage as Bérénice, Brown would summon up that scene on the dock to evoke her own feeling of abandonment.

"Barbara was the favorite all-time experience of my life, not just on stage, all my life," she told me. Brown's identification with Shaw's heroine goes far beyond anything I heard from other actors. Others spoke of their characters as spilling over briefly into their offstage lives, like Donnah Welby playing Lady Macbeth in the subway. But Brown said Major Barbara wrought a lasting change in her life. In the "long afterglow" of Barbara, she quit a waitressing job she'd held for twelve years. "It was debilitating," she recalled. "I was hiring myself out to be pushed around four, five nights a week, whenever I wasn't performing. I had money, I was comfortable, but I didn't have my soul, and when I was performing I was broke. Barbara wouldn't take that. Shaw created a character who wouldn't take less from life than she deserved. If it makes me lose everything, I'll only gain everything. So I walked out on that job on a Saturday night. I invited a friend to a Broadway play and bought the tickets with my last tips. I've never gone back." That was a year ago. Brown now gets by with voice coaching and temporary office work in addition to what she earns acting. "It's strange that it comes from a fictional character of a hundred years ago, but it's the only truth I know. It doesn't solve the world's problems, but it does solve mine. The sad thing, though, is to let go of such a fabulous source of inspiration. What would satisfy me the most in the whole world would be to do Major Barbara again. How happy I was! Every pore was filled."

We spoke for a while about how she shifts gears among her multiple roles in *The Trojan Women:* she plays in turn the goddess Athene, a nameless Trojan widow (as a member of the chorus), and the demigoddess Helen. Returning to her favorite role, Brown said: "I put Barbara in every play, and she's in this one too." She reminded me that Paris, Helen's abductor, is brought to her by a goddess. "Euripides has me say to Menelaus about Paris: 'He came with a goddess at his side; no weak one.' For me, that goddess is Barbara."

Joanne Camp is one of three actors who are playing in *Tartuffe* while rehearsing *The Trojan Women*. In the latter, she is Choragos, the leader of the three-woman chorus, and she is also understudying the enormously demanding role of Hecuba. The chorus itself is more demanding than it may seem, at least for a performer who asks as much of herself as Camp. She never carries the show, but she is on stage throughout and must sustain the mood of tragedy, though she seldom can express that emotion in words: if she fails to sustain the mood, the other actors are likely to be affected even if we in the audience don't notice it. Camp tells me she is finding it difficult to make the transition from Trojan tragedy to the comic world of Molière in the time available to her. Rehearsal ends at five; she begins at seven to prepare for Molière at eight, and in the interim she eats and rests. To help her get back into her other life as Orgon's wife, Camp writes a letter every evening to Elmire's brother, Cléante. She writes it in the dressing room in the last hour before the show. This is today's letter:

Dearest Cléante:

Now that you have returned from your travels in Scandinavia pls rush over—I regret that I cannot allow you time to resettle but we seem to have a "situation" on our hands. In brief Orgon has taken in a spiritual guide to live with us. I do not believe in his piety, but Orgon seems quite ready to do all this Monsieur Tartuffe advises. Needless to say, you will have no nieces or nephews if you do not come right away and help—speak to Orgon—you know how much he respects you and listens to you—as do I.

Hurry, my sweet
Your loving sister,
"Mire"

🦢 OCTOBER 7

The reviews of *Tartuffe* are in, and they aren't good.

The New York Times reviewed it twice, once in the daily and again in the Sunday paper. Neither reviewer liked the Pearl's production, though their reasons were somewhat contradictory. The daily complained of its "fast pacing," while Sunday's man found it "inert." The half dozen other reviews were mixed. The most favorable reviewer, Greg Evans in *Variety*, liked the staging of the play and singled out a "very funny" Julia Glander for her "comic skills" as the maid, Dorine.

Sobel observed to me, before the reviews came out, that present-day reviewers put opinion before reporting. In the past, he said, the writer would consider it his job first to tell the reader what the evening was about and what approach to the play was taken by those who staged it. Only then would he give his opinion of it. This distinction was drawn by the great Brooks Atkinson of the *Times*, who made a point of saying he was a reviewer, not a critic. Now, however, most writers follow what a friend once called (after the *New Yorker* film writer) the "Pauline Kael school of reviewing." These reviews read as if they should begin: "If I had directed this show . . ."

As I read over the eight reviews of *Tartuffe* it seemed to me that most of the writers, including both *Times* reviewers, fell into that second category of reviewing. They devoted so much space to their own opinions that there was little left to tell us about the show. I was reminded of the television reporter who stands in the middle of the screen describing a scene that we could see for ourselves if he would only get himself out of our way.

I noticed also that several writers were amazingly literal-minded. They wanted the modern analogues to the Tartuffe story driven into our skulls with a sledgehammer. I'd have thought the similarity of Tartuffe to our contemporary preacher-villains would be obvious to anyone who stayed awake through the show. But it wasn't obvious enough to suit the writer at the *Voice*, who complained of not "so much as a pro forma nod to the twentieth century," or the one at New York *Newsday*, who wanted a play about New York's Cardinal O'Connor. I imagined Tartuffe coming on stage with a name tag reading: HI! I'M JIMMY SWAGGART.

Reviews are less important to the Pearl than they are on Broadway, where a new show can live or die by the *Times* review. Off Broadway audiences, and especially those who attend a classical theatre such as the Pearl, are too knowledgeable to let the reviewer's opinion shape their own. They almost certainly know the playwright's work and often they are coming to see how this production compares with others they have seen. According to a survey the Pearl made last year, only 1 percent of the audiences said they came to the performance because of a review. It's a mature audience: more than half are past fifty, and one in five is retired. About one third are in the professions. In any event, more than half of the Pearl's audience is made up of subscribers, who have already signed up for the season. Still—Sobel tells me when we talk after the last review has come in—a favorable write-up in the *Times* can bring new spectators to the Pearl. So, for that matter, can a bad review, though of course in smaller numbers. It will draw a number of people who hadn't previously known the play was being shown and who are willing to make their own judgment of the production. Sobel believes these people outnumber those who were kept away by the unfavorable review.

"Our policy is to ignore the reviews," Sobel says. "Many theatres post good reviews in the lobby, but we never do. I only read them to find out how we'll do at the box office." There may be a bit of bravado in this, it strikes me, but it is of a piece with Sobel's refusal to collect celebrity quotes about the Pearl. The only reviewer this inner-directed man really values—and he says this often, in one way or another—is the spectator who can tell him that his life has been changed by the performance he just saw. Of course this is an impossible standard, but perhaps it is the only one worth having.

Sobel discourages the actors from reading reviews till the show has closed. In practice, however, most actors do read their reviews, and if they don't their friends will tell them what the reviewers are saying. "If I see that the morale of the cast is low because of a bad review, I have to try to deal with it," he says, "and if an actor lets his performance be affected, I'll send him a note about it."

Where reviews matter the most, I was surprised to learn, is not at the box office or with the actors—but with those who raise money for the theatre. Good press is part of the trustees' reward for the unpaid work they do for the theatre, and it's also a practical help in that work. "When a trustee asks a colleague at work to write a check to the Pearl, it helps a lot if he can show him a good write-up in the *Times*," Sobel tells me. "It also helps if our fund-raiser can send a good review along with an application to a foundation or a corporation."

Box office for *Tartuffe* has been "fair to good," Sobel says when I ask him to assess where the Pearl stands now that we are two months into the make-or-break season and this first play is two weeks from its closing. More people have seen *Tartuffe* than any previous Pearl production, although attendance is running about 10 percent below the goal Sobel set in his budget. Subscriptions, on the other hand, are exceeding the target. The Pearl has signed up forty more subscribers than the target of eight hundred. But only half of the budget comes from the box office, and contributions are lagging badly. (This is at least partly due to the death of Ivan Polley. A friend of the Pearl is filling in on a volunteer basis to keep applications moving while the staff looks for a new fund-raiser.)

"We're doing well, but we have a long way to go," Sobel sums up. I sense a note of disquiet in him that does not quite jibe with his professed optimism.

༄ OCTOBER 20

About thirty of us are gathered this Sunday noon around a horseshoe-shaped arrangement of tables in the back room of a Seventh Avenue bar and grill. It's the first of the season's post-mortem brunches, and the subject is *Tartuffe*, which ended its run last night.

The event is in part a fund-raiser: we pay thirty dollars for a ten-dollar meal. Also, and mostly, it's a rare opportunity for people who saw the play to meet and talk with the actors. Three of the actors and several trustees are present, and about twenty members of the audience. We've milled around for a while, and now we're eating dressed-up scrambled eggs and talking about Molière's play.

The idea is for everyone to have a say. Among those here is Alex Szogyi of Hunter College, a well-known Molière specialist, but Sobel is careful to avoid making it a listen-to-the-expert occasion, and Szogyi himself, though voluble enough, never pulls rank. The moderator goes around the table giving each of us a chance to sound off.

I soon see that those literal-minded reviewers need not have worried that the story's modern analogues would be lost on the audience. One person lightheartedly suggests that Molière was satirizing the recently concluded Senate hearings on the Supreme Court nomination of Clarence Thomas. Another is reminded of Sinclair Lewis's Elmer Gantry. Several people mention Jimmy Swaggart, which leads me to hope that someone somewhere will cast that marvelous character in an artistic mold that will give as much comic instruction to the future as Molière's Tartuffe does to us.

As I listen to the audience discuss the play we all saw, I am awed by the many meanings we find in Molière's apparently simple story. Actor Arnie Burton says it's about our need for a guru to guide us. Professor Szogyi believes it's about reason and unreason. I think it's about religion and the male ego. To Sobel it's not about religion but about Orgon's attempt to deal with the ground shifting under his feet. Could we all be right?

Across the table from me I see Julia Glander, our blond Dorine, who brought such comic energy to the play and such cheer to the weeks of rehearsal. I realize with regret that this is Glander's last appearance in our world: she's not a member of the company and she isn't scheduled for any more roles this season. This, I also realize, is part of theatre life. People work together under circumstances of great emotional intimacy for several weeks or months, then part, perhaps to meet someday on another stage, perhaps never to see each other again.

Sobel and I stay behind to talk when the others leave. His evaluation of *Tartuffe*, now that it's over, is about what it was on opening night: "The audience was usually pleased, but they didn't laugh till their sides hurt and we didn't prick at their consciences." Looking back, Sobel blames himself for not recasting the two main roles when he saw he was not going to get the performances he wanted from Martin LaPlatney and Frank Geraci. "We had two good actors and a director who didn't handle them effectively," he says with regret.

Of LaPlatney, Sobel says: "He brought a lot of energy to the show and a good performance attitude, and he did a valuable Tartuffe, but it wasn't the one I wanted. He wanted to make a clear Jimmy Swaggart. His Tartuffe could have lived in 1991, I wanted a Tartuffe set in 1669. Martin didn't even make a gesture to period style, he completely ignored the rhythm of movement Molière needs. He wanted to startle the audience, so he did comic bits that went over very well but detracted from the story. So we never told the story of the play.

"Frank never got the psychological truth of his character during rehearsal," Sobel says of Geraci's Orgon. "Being the conscientious actor he is, he kept on looking, and that took him away from the play as I directed it. Neither of us got what we wanted. Lots of evenings when he changed his performance he threw Dorine out of focus and the show fell flat." ("I kept looking for the truth in this guy, and I was grabbing at straws," Geraci said. "I couldn't adjust to the cartoon character Martin was playing. We were in two different plays." Geraci said he knew he and LaPlatney were "on the verge of being fired.")

So why, I ask Sobel, did he not replace those two actors? "In Martin's case I wasn't sure till it was about four days too late, and with Frank I wasn't sure till after the opening—much too late. I had no better choices available, and it could have been a lot worse. The lesson is to take a stronger hand sooner." He reflects a moment and adds: "It's a paradox. We're looking for strong performers who have a clear idea of what they're doing, but we also want the actors to fit that performance into the director's overall concept."

As he often does, Sobel puts the immediate experience into a longer perspective: "We're on the right track. Building a classical theatre takes thirty years with one company. It takes a dozen Molières. We're going about it right by bringing in Robert [Williams, the voice coach], Richard [Morse, who taught movement], and Dale [Ramsey, who ran a workshop in text analysis]. We learn a lot each time. This is a great profession, there's so much to learn. I keep learning. If I live long enough I'll be good at this."

☙ NOVEMBER 6

The Trojan Women is going into its second week when my wife, Janice, and I attend with two other couples.

Tonight's audience is very responsive. So, I find, am I: the story's power to move me is undiminished after seeing and hearing it half a dozen times. Donnah Welby's delivery of Andromache's great speech after the Greeks kill her son has me in tears once again along with everyone else in my row. (When I tell Sobel about my response to Welby's performance, he says: "Well, Euripides had something to do with it." The remark surprises me. It strikes me as both ungenerous and uncharacteristic of him. While accurate enough, he makes no such comment when I praise other performances of which the same could also be said.) Andromache's speech may be the tragic peak of the evening, but Bella Jarrett's Hecuba is on stage throughout and is the figure who carries the show. As I think about what goes into her performance, I recall Jarrett's saying that Hecuba is "King Lear for women." Late in the play, when Robin Leslie

Brown comes on as Helen, I am again impressed at how effectively this actress evokes her character's sensuality. A lot of that sensuality, my wife points out, is due to a costume designed to show off Brown's attractive shoulders and her satiny skin. Barbara Bell can do that because, as she says, "I know these bodies."

Much of the mood of the play seems to me due to designs that blend together successfully. The costumes differentiate the Trojans from the Greeks, and the gods from both. (Poseidon and Athene are in diaphanous garments lit to suggest they are naked. They are further set apart from mortals by appearing on the balcony over and behind the stage.)

"Shep wanted to show a highly cultured people who were not Western, not European, so that it was easier for the Greeks to justify destroying them," Barbara Bell told me during the tech week that precedes the opening. She was sitting erect at her sewing machine in the second-floor costume shop with a wall of shoes stuffed in cubbyholes behind her, and she was speaking in her usual direct, no-nonsense manner. "I studied the archeology, photos of the area, some artists' reconstructions. There's so little to go on, no clothing, a little pottery. It was a difficult creative process, a challenge that makes the brain work harder. I was looking for texture. I wanted an undefined Eastern look. What I came up with was loose-fitting garments of a brick color I got from the pottery. It was important also for the Trojan women's clothing to be of high quality, even though now, at the time of the play, when they're captives, it's in bad shape. These are women of the nobility. Hecuba is the King's widow. She's in rags now, but they have to be royal rags, not peasant ones."

The sound designed by Donna Riley was so subtle that, as Sobel observed, most people seeing the show were not even aware there *was* any sound. As Riley explained it to me, her purpose was to pitch her work in the narrow range where we are affected by sounds we are not consciously aware of hearing. She designed a mix of "environmental" sounds intended to reinforce the mood of what was happening on stage. For the victorious Greeks, preparing to sail home, she mixed the sound of the sea, the cry of gulls, the clatter of people on shipboard, all below our conscious awareness, and she concentrated the sound in the speakers behind the audience to suggest the direction of the sea. For the defeated Trojans, excluded from that lively activity, there was the lonely sound of the wind, and for Andromache, seeing her murdered son carried off on her husband Hector's shield, the call of a vulture. "That's when she has to let go of her son and her heritage," Riley observed. "It would have been overstated to use that sound when he was killed." For the killing scene she used a transition from the Greeks' ocean to the Trojans' wind. Riley preferred silence to even the most subtle sound at two times during the play: for the gods in the opening scene, and when Helen is trying to win back Menelaus.

The sound was difficult both to design and to operate. Not only must its volume be within a narrow range to achieve the right effect—a little higher and it distracts us from the action, a little lower and we miss it entirely—but that right pitch will change with the number of people in the audience and whether the heating system is on. Colleen Davis, the apprentice stage manager, said later that operating Riley's design from the backstage sound board was her hardest job of the season. In place of the one tape used for *Tartuffe* Davis had to keep three tapes going with Riley's cues for mixing the hundred-odd sounds she had put on the tapes. Davis frequently had to vary the volume of the various speakers to suggest the different directions from which the sound was coming, and she had to adjust the sound level at each performance for the heating or lack of it and for the size of the audience.

It was worth it, according to Sobel, who thinks the sound makes a valuable contribution to the show. "She did a great job," he says that evening after the show. "She gave us a mood and a texture with a design that supported what the actors were doing without ever making a point of itself. This is what all design is supposed to do." Sobel says the importance of the sound was brought home to him when the show had to go on without it for two performances because of a broken amplifier.

"Both the actors and I were very conscious of its loss, though when it was there we were never aware of it."

Our conversation now turns to a favorite Sobel topic: the need for the actor to stretch in performance. To me there's a touch of the Puritan in this, the no-pain, no-gain notion that if it doesn't hurt, there's something missing. Sobel, however, believes that's why people come to the theatre, for the tension of seeing actors attempting the difficult, not to see them show off easy mastery. "If we want to be lulled, stay home and watch the tube, because television is a lulling medium." Sobel draws on another of his many analogies. "It's like sports photography," he tells me. "The best sports photos always show the athlete in the act of stretching himself, reaching for the ball, aiming for distance with the javelin. The excitement is in our uncertainty about whether he'll succeed, whether he'll catch the ball or make the distance. The same is true of the actor. We want to see him reach for the goal, and if it's too easy there's not going to be any reach for us to see. It'll be a less interesting performance."

We got on that subject after I reported my group's reaction to the company's performance in *The Trojan Women*. We'd all praised Donnah Welby's Andromache and Robin Leslie Brown's Helen. Sobel calls my attention to the unusual casting of those two roles. "Robin's not an easy choice for Helen," he points out. "The natural casting is Helen for Donnah and Andromache for Robin. If we'd done the usual thing, they'd both have been more comfortable in their roles. They wouldn't have been stretched and their performances would have been less interesting—good, but less interesting." I recall now that several of the actors mentioned the untypical parts they'd been given as one of the reasons they liked working at the Pearl. "Only in a theatre with a resident company can you do that kind of casting," Sobel adds.

Arnie Burton's Talthybius is a different case of stretch. Talthybius is the Greek soldier-messenger who informs the Trojan women of their respective fates, and who reluctantly follows his orders and takes Andromache's son off to be killed. "Arnie's a fine actor, but physically he's wrong for Talthybius," my wife observed, and we all agreed. We imagined Talthybius as a battle-scarred warrior who has no qualms about killing men in combat; that, we thought, gave poignancy to his disgust at having to kill a child. Arnie Burton has the fresh and innocent look of someone who's never been near a battlefield. At thirty-three, he's old enough for the role, but you can't look at his face and believe it of him, and that's what matters. Sobel observes that nothing in the play identifies Talthybius as a front-line soldier and he says: "We tried to toughen Arnie up as much as possible." Burton went without shaving, but a dark, stubbly chin wasn't enough to transform that face. He looked like an innocent youth who needed a shave. Sobel concedes the point and then says: "It would be easy to cast Arnie in roles he's just right for. He's an easy actor to cast. But that's not enough. We need to develop actors who can do anything."

"Isn't that asking too much of them?"

Sobel, I am again reminded, is adept at converting my question into his answer. "We're looking for actors we can ask too much of," he now says, with just an edge of laughter in his voice at the way he's appropriating my question. "We're the only theatre I know that's doing that, and I think it's what we should be doing. It's at a cost. We have to take some risks. That's what we did when we cast Arnie as Talthybius. It's worth taking those risks for the future of the actors and the company."

NOVEMBER 11

Rosalind in Shakespeare's *As You Like It* is Joanne Camp's favorite role. She's played her twice, and she's been waiting almost ten years for an opportunity to play her again. She'll start that third time tomorrow when the Pearl's production of *As You Like It* goes into rehearsal.

"My first Rosalind was in college, and it was the first Shakespeare I ever did," she tells me. "I did it again when Shep directed a Shakespeare festival in West Virginia in 1983. I was one of only three professional actors in that one." We are in the two-room apartment on West Twenty-fifth Street to which she and Sobel recently moved from the cramped but cheap one-room quarters in Hell's Kitchen they'd lived in for many years. It's late afternoon on her one day off of the week; we're facing each other across a coffee table on which Camp has put out a plate of cookies and grapes that we are nibbling. "It's very exciting to come back to Rosalind after all these years," she says. She is smiling and her manner is calmly gracious. At times like this, Camp seems more like a Southern hostess—she's from Georgia—than an actress, though, it also occurs to me, this may be a role she plays particularly well. She's known around the Pearl for her hot temper—I felt its heat myself on one occasion—but she otherwise shows none of the outward theatricality that we tend to expect from her profession.

"I'm very nervous about feeling I'm too old for Rosalind, that I've waited too long. Maybe I'm just being silly, but since I turned forty last year I've gotten very age-conscious. I've been driving Shep and Arnie crazy talking about getting a face-lift." Arnie Burton, who is thirty-three, will play her lover, Orlando. Shakespeare doesn't give their ages; they are inexperienced young people whom today we would see as being in their early twenties. "Still, others have played Rosalind when they were older than I am—I looked them all up!—and there's a good reason for actors to play roles that are ten or fifteen years younger than they are. They've been there, they've lived through that age, and now they have some perspective on it. It's far different from playing a character who's older than you.

"I know I have a lot to bring to it. Rosalind will allow me to bring together everything I've learned since I last played her. My work used to be very emotional, very much based on instinct. That's because I was poorly trained and didn't know how else to go about it. Since then my work has veered over almost too much to the technical side, to the sound of my voice, to the architectural build of a scene, rather than focusing on, What is this person trying to accomplish, what is she trying to get from the other person on stage with her? Now, with more intelligence"—she laughs—"at least I hope I've got more, I can make choices from an intellectual base also. It's a perfect opportunity for me to marry those two." She pauses. "We were talking about that today at the theatre—do you approach the part from a technical or emotional angle? I think you go back and forth."

Camp has found a model for Rosalind right in the theatre's tiny upstairs office, in the person of Janine Lindsay, the tall young British woman who is in her second year as a management apprentice at the Pearl. "I don't go back to my younger self so much as I look at other young women, and Jan strikes me as very Roz-like," she says. "She has very mercurial moods, one moment happy, the next desperately unhappy. But she's true to every emotion, she doesn't give it up easily. And she always knows just how she feels." Again she stops to reflect. "Well, I'm using her in my preparation. I'm not sure how much it'll pay off in rehearsal." Camp also carries with her a picture of her seventeen-year-old niece to remind her of that age.

"I'm happy to be doing it this time with all professional actors," Camp says, and now her thoughts turn to the Pearl company, who will all be in *As You Like It* except Frank Geraci. "The way I act best is with someone who's demanding something from me. That's why I'm so excited about working with Arnie. He demands from others and he gives to them. Robin [Leslie Brown] very much gives to you also. We'd be a lot further along as a company if everyone put in the effort and energy that Arnie and Robin do." She has mixed praise and criticism for the two other men in the company, Geraci and Stuart Lerch. But, in this and other conversations, Camp either ignores the two remaining members, Donnah Welby and Laura Rathgeb, or makes observations about them that are invariably negative.

Camp returns to Rosalind to say: "I've seen about eleven

productions, including Maggie Smith's, but I've never seen it totally done. I want to do it totally."

I ask whether playing *The Trojan Women* gets in the way of preparing for Rosalind. She says: "No, I'm so excited about Rosalind that *The Trojan Women* helps hold me in check. Without it, I might devour everyone in sight." A bit later, however, she turns serious and says: "It's been wearing on all of us, all the Trojan women. It's a challenge to get yourself into that emotional state every night. Your body and your emotions rebel, and you have to be more wily in accessing the feelings you need. I think about my Trojan husband and all my brothers being killed, and images of my own brother flash through my mind." Her mood changes again, and she says something that to me sums up the fascination of the actor's work for those of us who spend our lives confined within the four walls of our own identities. Camp smiles as she says it, but her intent is clearly serious: "It's been a marvelous experience. After all, how often does an actor get a chance to be that unhappy?"

NOVEMBER 23

"Shepherd Sobel makes some deep cuts—principally in the chants of the chorus. . . . People who know the original will miss some of the sweeping choral odes. . . ." So writes D. J. R. Bruckner, the *New York Times* reviewer.

That startled me, and not because he misspelled Sobel's first name, Shepard. I knew Sobel's respect for the author's text, and I'd heard no discussion of cuts during rehearsal. Sobel told me he cut just four words, a reference to "you men" when the Pearl production was only providing one man (the man or men in question are nonspeaking walk-ons). Had the *Times* man asked him about the supposed cuts? No, Sobel said, he had heard nothing from the *Times*.

I called Bruckner at the *Times* and asked him about the "deep cuts." Bruckner said he had thought while attending the play that passages were missing in the odes. He said he had not read the play in preparation for reviewing it but that he knew the Greek original well from his undergraduate days. "I remembered there were some things people said that I didn't hear, so when I went home I checked to make sure in the book that's in the hallway when I go in the door," he said.

"Maybe the translator made the cuts," Bruckner added. "I had no way of knowing." There was, of course, a very easy way of finding out, and it seemed to me that any responsible journalist would have checked with Sobel before reporting as fact that Sobel had made those "deep cuts."

If there were any cuts. Two Greek scholars, John Marry and Nancy Langalin (who wrote her dissertation on Euripides), had also thought after seeing it that there might be cuts in the Pearl production. They told me they checked the Greek original against the translation used by the Pearl (by Richmond Lattimore) and against their memories—and found that nothing at all was missing.

(It should be said here that the *Times*, to its great credit, prints many more reviews of Off and Off Off Broadway productions than any comparable publication. That matters far more than the instances of irresponsible journalism.)

Sobel explained why one might think he'd cut the text of the odes. "He [the *Times* reviewer] was probably expecting the odes to be songs spoken by a group, separate interludes that don't seem part of the play. The odes are usually the most obscure part of it. What he got was choral speaking that made sense to the play, so he didn't identify it as part of the odes. We didn't change anything, the difference is all in how it's done. It's the same reaction we often get when we do Shakespeare. People will say: 'You really updated it!' That's because they could understand everything, so they think we must have changed the text." He shrugged, then smiled as he found the ironic point of the event: "We made it understandable. To me that says we did a good job. To Mr. Bruckner it says we made deep cuts."

DECEMBER 2

Sobel's aims for this season are beginning to look overly optimistic. At a Monday-night board meeting, a dozen of us sitting around on the stage before the set of *The Trojan Women* hear that income is falling below budget by about twenty thousand dollars. Not a huge amount, but unless it picks up, the Pearl's stay on Off Broadway will be cut short.

Neither the box office nor fund-raising is meeting its target. *The Trojan Women* is drawing far fewer spectators than *Tartuffe*, even though, as Sobel tells us, it and Shakespeare's *Pericles* are the only classics now playing in New York. Ivan Polley's death deprived the Pearl of its professional fund-raiser and it also cast a pall over the tiny upstairs office in which he and the three other members of the staff worked at quarters that were very close emotionally as well as physically. His replacement, Larry Auld, reports on the applications he's been getting out to foundations, but very little money is coming in. In this circumstance, a trustee comes up with a rather macabre idea. Let's try to find new trustees from the boards of the all too many theatres that have gone under recently. Like most such institutions, the Pearl is always on the lookout for new trustees willing to give their time and money, and people who've just had their favorite theatre shot out from under them would seem excellent prospects. Sobel says it would look like "dirty pool," and the idea drifts away.

The Pearl is not likely to find a new home soon. The capital campaign to finance a new theatre died with Ivan Polley, and no one is much taken with the one place that's been seriously considered. (Weeks earlier I'd gone with a Pearl group to examine that possibility. It was a much larger, but uninviting, space on West Thirty-sixth Street. Set designer Robert Joel Schwartz prowled the stage, muttering to himself, while Donna Riley, the sound designer, moved from place to place, clapping and listening for the echo. As we were leaving, she told me she'd found nothing about the sound that ruled out the site, but that she'd have to come again to be sure: this was a preliminary examination.) Still, the Pearl will need more space if it is to stay on Off Broadway: its present theatre just doesn't have enough seats to bring in the income it will need to meet its higher budget. My wife spoke for many of us when she asked Sobel: "Why would you want to leave this charming place?" "Do you want to pay sixty dollars for a ticket?" he asked in turn.

Should the Pearl avoid staging tragedies in these depressing times, one trustee wonders aloud, thinking of the poor box office for *The Trojan Women*. No, Alice Tierstein, the house choreographer, says firmly, "we need *more* tragedy in hard times." She is Sobel's cousin, but the family resemblance is so marked—the curly black hair and full lips, the look of good-humored intelligence—that she could easily be his sister.

Before we get down to the business of business, the trustees hear from the director of *As You Like It*, now in rehearsal. It's one of Sobel's ways of bringing the trustees into the artistic as well as the fiscal life of the theatre. Most artistic directors keep trustees well away from the stage for fear they'll start imposing ideas of their own. Sobel, however, believes that trustees who know the life of the theatre as well as its balance sheet will be more motivated to support it; and that's worth an occasional case of backseat driving. So, at every board meeting, the trustees listen to, and question, a director or designer or actor talking about some aspect of the theatre's work.

Today it's Anthony Cornish. He's a British director, and when you hear his BBC voice, and you see his silver hair over a high brow, his blue eyes and long English jaw—you know that he fits the part perfectly. When I remarked on this to Sobel, he smiled and said: "Well, I cast him for it, didn't I?"

Cornish, a free lance who lives in London, is directing his third production at the Pearl. He's not here for the money ($1,500 for six weeks, plus a couple of days' preparation with the costume and set designers), but neither is anyone else, except possibly the plumber. Cornish comes for the artistic freedom of Sobel's "loose but firm hand on the reins," because he likes the Pearl company, and for the plays he gets to direct. (His previous productions were *Major Barbara* and *The Importance of Being Earnest.*) He's staying in Frank Geraci's apartment while Geraci is doing a play in Hartford. He came to New York on his way to direct a show in Florida, which is why he is able to come at all, and after that he'll go on to a theatre in Luxembourg.

That afternoon, sitting in the first row of the empty theatre, I ask Cornish about the supposed differences between American and British actors. We always hear, I say, that American actors work with emotion, the British with technique. "That's precisely untrue," says Cornish, precisely enunciating every syllable. When I ask about the common belief that American actors can't speak well enough to do Shakespeare, he says: "That's *more* precisely untrue. There's a received wisdom among American actors that verges on an inferiority complex about their ability to be vocally expressive. I don't think many British actors feel that way about themselves. The balance of it is that Americans have an ability to fling themselves physically at a task." Cornish has directed Shakespeare twenty-odd times on both sides of the language barrier. "I wouldn't think of doing *As You Like It* in English English," he says, and he goes on with great diplomacy: "I think the American language is a rich one. There's some snobbery among the British about Americans playing Shakespeare, but, on the other hand, London welcomed Dustin Hoffman doing Shylock."

But there is a considerable economic gap between actors on the two sides of the Atlantic. Actors at a British equivalent of the

Pearl—actors of similar skill and experience—would be 50 percent better off than their American counterparts, Cornish said. They could get by on their pay without working at other jobs. What makes the difference, I realize, is that the British are far more committed to live performance than are we Americans.

Later that day I ask Sobel to compare his and Cornish's directing styles. "Tony allows the actor to find the interpretation of the character with which he's most comfortable. Obviously, it has to be within the parameters of the lines and Tony has to harmonize that actor's performance with the others'. Within those limits, though, Tony seeks the actor's maximum comfort. But I tend to push the actor to the edge of his range, to make him stretch, and that puts him in a zone of minimum comfort." He laughs. "It's a hallmark of Tony's shows that at least ninety percent of the actors are delighted to be working with him."

〰️ DECEMBER 3

High rent makes for strange bedfellows: the gym we're in is also a Buddhist temple. On the floor in front of us lies a mat, and at the far wall I can see an Eastern-looking altar. As we enter we're asked to remove our shoes, which, it occurs to me, could be for either athletic or religious reasons.

We—two Pearl actors with me tagging along—are here for a first rehearsal with the fight choreographer. In *As You Like It*, Orlando, played by Arnie Burton, first attracts Rosalind by defeating the evil Duke's champion wrestler. The latter is portrayed by Alex Leydenfrost, a young actor who has been playing small parts at the Pearl for little pay and for credits toward membership in Actors' Equity.

One look is enough to tell you that this match is David versus Goliath—and in Shakespeare's account the little guy has no slingshot. Our hero, Burton's Orlando, is slender and delicate. He is giving away seven years, seven inches of height, and no less than sixty pounds to the powerfully built Leydenfrost. It will be hard to maintain illusion in this fight, the actors point out to me as we're walking over from the Pearl. The trickery and reshooting that can be done with film isn't available, and in the small Pearl the spectators can see the action on stage much better than in a Broadway house.

The fight choreographer, Rick Sordelet, asks Burton and Leydenfrost to strip to their shorts and starts them on some warming-up exercises. The actors are working on the mat; I'm sitting by the wall trying to stay out of everyone's way. While loosening up, Sordelet says to me: "Don't expect to see much choreographing today. This first session is mainly to establish trust between Arnie and Alex, and for me to find out what they can and can't do. Then I'll design the fight within those limits and in keeping with their characters." Sordelet has the actors doing rolls together on the mat. Then, up on their feet, they're throwing each other against the gym wall. They stop for a moment's rest, and Sordelet talks to them about fitting the action to their characters. "I want to show in your opening moves that Orlando knows the rules of the game," he says. He asks Burton how the fight should end. "According to the lines, it's not a knockout," Burton says. "I think Alex is semiconscious."

I slip out still unconvinced that Burton can win what will seem to us in the audience an honest fight.

Back at the Pearl, I find that the rest of the cast is being tested in a different way—a singing coach is trying out their voices. This production of *As You Like It*, which has a lot of singing in it, will use music written for the Royal Shakespeare Company. Young Hank Wagner will go back to his early teenage career as a vocalist to sing a big solo as Hymen, the god of marriage, and the whole company will sing the finale. "We'll be singing a capella"—groans from the cast—"with as much harmony as we can muster," says director Anthony Cornish.

The voice coach asks who has had singing instruction—all but two of the dozen actors raise their hands. When he groups them by voice, they all know which part they should sing. Some fight, others sing: I marvel once again at the variety of physical skills that go into being an actor.

During the lunch break I ask Joanne Camp about Blanda's, the restaurant at the end of the block. She gives me a dazzling smile and says, not even remotely in answer to my question: "I always order the cheapest pasta, but if you"—her voice caresses the pronoun—"if *you* took me there on your expense account, I'd order the most expensive dish on the menu!" She bats her eyelashes at me, laughs like a teenager, and glides gracefully away. I stare after her in disbelief. This is not the Joanne Camp I know. The one I know is gracious and serious, sometimes moody and hot-tempered—she is never flirtatious. While I am puzzling over this event, I recall what has just happened and the explanation comes to me. I'm seeing that spilling over of the role into offstage life that other actors have described to me. Just before lunch, Camp's Rosalind was sitting on a tree stump, leaning back soulfully and saying to her lover Orlando: "Woo me!"

That was Rosalind flirting with me! Knowing that gives me a strange feeling.

Stuart Lerch—Poseidon and Menelaus in *The Trojan Women*—is playing Jaques, who says he loves melancholy better than laughing. Lerch tells me he likes the role, and certainly the melancholy Jaques suits the tall, gaunt Lerch, who when he is not rehearsing often looks as if he is lost in a private and melancholy world of his own. Jaques has one of the most famous of Shakespeare's speeches, the one about the seven ages of man that begins: "All the world's a stage . . . " I ask Lerch if he anticipates having trouble giving the speech without sounding as if he were reciting from *Bartlett's Familiar Quotations*. "Not at all," he says. "I think of it as fresh out of the typewriter, written just for me."

Late that afternoon I am in the yard eating a persimmon with a couple of actors when Laura Rathgeb, usually so reticent and serious of manner, bursts out the back door exclaiming: "David! We've been talking about your book in the dressing room, and we've got a title for it!" While she pauses for dramatic effect I wonder what can possibly be coming my way. She says, "It's what we're most often asked: *How Do You Remember All Those Lines?*"

☙ DECEMBER 21

"This is the longest I'll be away in season since we first opened the theatre, and I'm frantic about it," Sobel says as we're walking up Seventh Avenue. It's late afternoon and we're going to his apartment to talk during the five o'clock Saturday show that is a Pearl innovation. The theatre will be closed for three days over Christmas. Sobel and Joanne Camp will visit his brother in Hartford, and he is worrying about who will watch over his Pearl while he is away.

I soon learn that Sobel has much more on his mind than a three-day absence. "This is a very tough week," Sobel begins when we're sitting in his apartment with a bottle of red wine between us. He's slouched on the sofa, and even if I hadn't heard the words I'd know it was a tough time from the tenor of his voice. He's not maintaining his usual style, that outward composure of a gentleman at the court of Louis XIV which I've come to expect of him; he's tired and discouraged and he doesn't care if I see it. "I really expected that *As You Like It* would be selling out and it's not. This show has to pick up and pick up fast, or we're in trouble."

I became aware that afternoon that the Pearl's plight was far more serious than I had realized. Mary Harpster, the quiet and unflappable general manager who knows all the numbers, took me through those figures in the tiny upstairs office. Her conclusion was that the theatre was going to run out of cash in less than two weeks. The Pearl's expenses were higher than they'd ever been. The payroll was at a record level: fourteen actors in *As You Like It* plus five actors rehearsing the next show, Ibsen's *Ghosts* (but two were in both shows, a back-to-back that saved the Pearl part of each of their salaries). What's more, the payroll had to be met every week on time; Harpster could not juggle the payroll as she often does the Con Ed and some other bills. Then there's three thousand dollars a month in taxes, and, she said, "the Federal government charges very nasty interest if you're late." So what happens if the cash runs dry? Harpster explained the ways of getting by. ART/New York, the service organization for Off and Off Off Broadway theatres, has a loan fund from which the Pearl could borrow on the strength of a letter from a foundation saying it expects to give the theatre a grant in the spring. But if nothing else happens in the interim that loan only postpones the income gap to the spring, or to the next season—if there *is* a next season. For the first time I'm beginning to wonder about that.

"We're halfway through the season, box office isn't holding up, and I'm not sure why," Sobel is saying. "The first show [*Tartuffe*] came in ten percent short because of the reviews. We'd started out selling very well before the *Times* panned us twice. *The Trojan Women* came in a good thirty percent off. I don't think that was because of the reviews, which I took to be mixed. I don't know what it was. Of course we're trying to sell a lot more seats now, and it's true that more people saw *The Trojan Women* than ever saw a Pearl production in any other year, but that doesn't help us now." What can he do to sell those extra seats, I ask. "I could cast a couple of stars to bring people to the box office, but I'm not willing to do that." I've known that ever since he told me in one of our earliest conversations that "we're militantly anti-star." Thinking I'd found a chink in his moral armor, I observe that the *Times* listing of the current show reads: "Joanne Camp stars in Shakespeare's *As You Like It*." "That's the *Times*, not us," Sobel says. "I did *not* send in anything saying 'stars.' " His voice rises on a sudden note of asperity, and I realize he is reacting to my suggestion that he bent his principles for his wife. He quickly recovers his equanimity and goes on a bit sheepishly: "Well, maybe I let it slip by, but I'd like to think it [the offending word "stars"] was added by whoever at the paper edited our press release for the listings."

And if the "serious trouble" the Pearl is now in continues to the end of the season—what then? "We'd have to make major changes. We don't have a significant deficit now. You don't get that kind of deficit at $180,000 [the Pearl's budget a couple of seasons ago] because you're fairly sure of $160,000 of it. But at $380,000 [the budget for the current season]—yes, you can. I don't want to carry the kind of deficit we're facing into another season. I have real questions about what we'll do if we have a serious deficit." He pauses and frowns into his wineglass as if reading omens. "We don't have an awful lot of choices. We can't say we'll do only three-character plays [to save on actors' salaries] because they didn't write three-character plays." I ask about going back to the Pearl's previous status as a low-budget Off Off Broadway theatre. "You can't make up a deficit when you're limited [by Equity rules] to twenty-four performances and twelve-dollar tickets. Besides, it's hard on fund-raising to say we're taking a step backwards." It would be hard on everyone's morale, including Sobel's, I realize. When he resumes, his tone is emphatic. "I don't want to be a different kind of theatre. I don't want to be a theatre at any cost. I want to be a classical theatre." I sense what's coming next, but it's still a surprise because it's the first time I've heard Sobel suggest this possibility in our many hours together over the past year: "We'd have to fold up shop."

◥ DECEMBER 28

"They don't tell you in school about the business of acting," Arnie Burton said the first time we met. "Even if they had, I wouldn't have believed it." Donnah Welby, one day in the Pearl office, told me she was thinking of taking a course in the business of acting. "Getting work, the business side of acting, that's how we spend seventy-five percent of our time," she said. "The work itself, the acting, that's the frosting on the cake." Eventually I was able to talk to both members of the Pearl company about the business of their careers.

Arnie Burton, now thirty-three, came to New York ten years ago with only two years of professional experience. "Sometimes I've made a living as an actor, but more of the time I haven't," he says of those ten years. We're sitting at a table in the Pearl's upstairs costume shop. This place is humming and overcrowded when Barbara Bell is cutting costumes and fitting them to actors' bodies. But Bell is not here today, so the shop is deserted and oddly silent: the costumes hang waiting for actors to bring them back to life on the stage.

Burton's New York career got off to a fast start when he understudied the title role in *Amadeus* on Broadway and played the part on the road for, all told, about a year. I can see him in the part: his boyish good looks seem ideally suited to the young Mozart. "It was wonderful money, the most I've ever made in my life, before or since," he says.

"This is easy, this is the way it's going to be all of the time, I told myself." He laughs ruefully. "Of course it didn't happen that way. I had a long dry spell. I wasn't getting any work at all. My confidence was slipping lower and lower. I'd forgotten why I was here. I was a mass of insecurities, and it showed in my auditions.

It was affecting my work." He stops a moment. "It happens to a lot of young actors. They come to this city, they have no notion how to do an audition. So they're free, they're themselves. Then they learn how the business works, what the casting director is, what an agent is, and they get paranoid. They try to guess what the casting director wants and give him that in the audition, they try to be what an agent wants. They lose the special quality that is their own unique self. Blandness creeps in. We give away so many parts of ourselves to please others that there's nothing left. That's what happened to me. When I did an audition I didn't play it the way I saw it, so I didn't project the special quality that's Arnie, which is all that makes Arnie interesting as an actor. I'd lost what gave me my first success."

Burton is leaning across the bare table and talking with great earnestness: "I realized I had to do something! I remember the day. I was doing nothing, living off unemployment and savings from *Amadeus*. I was lying around all day, sleeping and watching television. I got up and went out to a bookstore, and"—he gives me an apologetic glance—"it's almost a cliché, but I bought a copy of Norman Vincent Peale's *The Power of Positive Thinking*. That led me to a spiritual path, and I began studying Yoga, Eastern religions, I read Emerson's essay on self-reliance. The power of the self, that was the message of everything I read. I didn't know who I was anymore. I had to get myself back." He says his acting teacher was the other influence that helped him get his acting back on track. "She taught me how to find what's special about Arnie, what I can bring to a role. But it's a slow process, and it's still going on."

Burton then spent four years waiting tables at the Museum Café on Columbus Avenue: "I was living the cliché, the actor who waits tables in a restaurant. It's a real trap, the money's so good, you get to do things you can never do on actor's pay. I know a lot of actors who've gotten lazy. They still call themselves actors, not waiters, but they never act, they never even go out on auditions." Like Robin Leslie Brown, who quit waitressing under the influence of Major Barbara, Burton knew he had to get out of that restaurant. "I was so proud of myself when I quit waiting tables! It showed I was in charge of my life. If I want to act I can." That was in 1989. Since then Burton hasn't held a job that required him to work during the run of a show. To make that possible, he works at odd jobs during summers and between shows. Over the years he's walked dogs for the Elite Dog Service, cleaned buildings, painted and plastered and cleaned apartments. Sometimes on his weekly day off he paints an apartment, for which—here again the awful economics of acting—he'll earn as much as the Pearl pays him per week. Otherwise, however, he lives on "a really strict budget. It's exhausting living on so little."

He turns to the experiences of other actors he knows. "Some friends who never get acting jobs envy me even though my pay's so meagre. On the other hand, a friend of mine just got on a soap and she's making literally thousands a week." I pose the obvious question. "Don't ask!" Burton says with a laugh. "Sure, I'd swap with her, but just for a short time to pile up some money, then I'd want to come back to this. I'm doing roles I love with people I love."

I ask Burton what are his realistic hopes for the future: "If I could have the best of both worlds, I'd do an occasional small role in a movie or television, because that's where the money is. Then I could afford to stay in New York, and I do love this city. I'd stay at the Pearl. I never want to get too far away from this place, but I have to get away now and then." Like most actors I've come to know this year, Burton believes he has to improve his business skills: "I'm a naive businessman. I need to work on enjoying auditions, on going to parties, meeting people, keeping my name before casting directors and agents. It's so easy to cocoon up. But I've got to get out there and push myself. This is a business!"

I find Donnah Welby in the women's dressing room. She is reclining on a couch in a baggy sweatshirt and pants. With her dark-haired good looks and self-assured manner, Welby reminds me of an off-duty Cleopatra, an image she plays with while we

talk by occasionally striking a mock-seductive pose for the enter-
tainment of other actresses wandering in and out of the dressing
room.

Musing about her career, Welby quotes Robert Frost on the
road not taken. The road she forsook was the one leading to a
lasting personal relationship. "You can't have it all, personal and
professional," she reflects. "I think it's a choice women face more
than men. You have to stick with the relationship or take the
tour." She means that literally: acting assignments that took her
out of New York for months on end, once for a full year. "I've
had very good relationships that fell apart because I took the
tour. It's hard to keep a long-distance relationship going, especially when you're young and stupid. Actually, any relationship
outside the business is difficult. It's not easy for a lawyer, say, to
see his wife or girlfriend necking with someone else on stage in
front of everyone and working Saturday night and Sunday."
Welby erupts into her raucous laugh.

Welby took the road from Washington, where she was well
established as an actress, to "go for the gold" in New York. That
was more than ten years ago, and she hasn't yet found the gold.
In Washington she worked steadily on stage and made her living
as an actress with only occasional side jobs as a convention
hostess or cocktail waitress. "In retrospect, maybe I should have
stayed in Washington," she says. "I'd probably have done more
theatre and I could have had a solid career. But I had to reach
for the brass ring." After a moment's thought she corrects herself: "I'm not really sorry I did it. I like New York a lot better
than Washington."

Her life in New York is divided between acting, mostly at the
Pearl, and her full-time executive position at the Theatre Development Fund. She's worked on soaps for brief stretches, and
she's done occasional commercials, but always she's depended
on TDF to pay the rent. Once Welby went to Los Angeles with
a film director she knew and tried to break into the film business.
It didn't pan out. "I wasn't getting any work," she says. "The

relationship broke up and I was broke. It was either work at Taco Bell for a couple of years and hope something would happen, or come back here."

With her life half over—"Well, not really!" she interrupts herself with that explosive laugh—Welby feels that she's at a turning point. "The question is, what do I do with the rest of my life? I'd like to leave my job at TDF. I don't want to spend thirty-five hours a week supervising others. I could take the plunge. I don't have three kids and a mortgage, so I'd be hurting no one but myself. It might make the difference for me. Sometimes if you remove the safety net—TDF in my case—you work a lot harder to make something happen." I ask what would make her decide to take that plunge. Welby answers in a very quiet tone: "It's a leap of faith."

When she continues, the note of playful mockery that often characterizes Welby's conversation is missing from her voice: "I'm ready for a break. I've laid the groundwork for it. My career's been a series of building blocks. Now I really know what it takes to be an actress and I know how to do it. I know how to press my own buttons, I'm not dependent on a director or a producer or another actor. I'm in control of it. If I ever got a break, I could do well with it." I'm reminded once again that this is a profession where talent and hard work are not enough, not when a hundred other equally experienced actors turn out for every audition and the choice depends on how the director feels that day. An actor has to do everything right and be lucky besides. That's what Welby is saying when she says: "Breaks have not been a part of my past. It would be nice to have one in my future."

ᐁᔓ JANUARY 3

"Tony Randall doing a Feydeau farce? Where does he get off coming in with his million dollars he made in a TV sitcom saying, 'Now we're going to do the classics'? It's such a damned insult. I'm furious at him. I'd punch him in the nose if I had him here." I was astonished at the vehemence in Sobel's voice. In the year I'd known him, I'd seen him maintain his smiling courtesy through the stress of one crisis after another, and on the single occasion I saw him briefly lose his self-control it was not to anger but to sorrow, over the death of Ivan Polley. I'd once asked Mary Harpster, who has sat across a small desk from him every working day for five years, when she last saw Sobel lose his temper. Harpster had remained silent, frowning in concentration, and finally said: "There was one time with a mechanic . . ." When was that? Again she frowned, and said uncertainly: "I think it was about three years ago, maybe four."

The occasion for Sobel's anger was my question about the enormous burst of publicity generated over Tony Randall's announcement that he'd raised six million dollars for an American classical repertory theatre, which his brochure compared to, among others, the Moscow Art Theatre and the Comédie-Française. Randall's National Actors Theatre would present, the brochure also said, "America's finest actors" in "civilization's greatest plays."

"He's going to start with *The Crucible,* a deeply American play, and he brings in a director who's barely lived in America," Sobel said. "Then he's going to do the Feydeau with a bad movie actor who's never stepped on a stage. It's an indication of such ignorance of what it takes to do theatre. Unfortunately all the work that real stage actors and classical actors are doing will take a step backwards." What most angered Sobel, I knew, was that Randall's public statements, and his casting decisions, showed no appreciation for the training that Sobel believes is necessary to stage the classics: Randall's theatre appears to have no equivalent to the workshops in speech and movement and text analysis the Pearl provides its company. As he often does, Sobel illustrated his point with an analogy from the world of sports: "Nobody would say, I haven't played any tennis in ten years, and I wasn't much good when I did, but I think I'll go join the [professional] tour. That's what he's doing."

Sobel concluded, still in anger: "I hope he falls flat on his face. But I hope the critics say: 'The reason this failed is not because this is what classics are. It's because nobody pays any respect to what it takes to do the classics.' "

That conversation was four months ago. Now, when we return to the topic Sobel can talk about Randall's efforts with his usual good humor. When I remind him of his initial reaction, he smiles a bit ruefully and says: "I'm sure there was a good deal of sour grapes in that. I wish there'd been some recognition of the work we've been doing here for eight years." Though he never says it, the thought must have crossed his mind, as it did mine, that the six million dollars raised for the National Actors Theatre would have provided Sobel's dream theatre with the resources he would need to do the classics right, instead of being wasted on Tony Randall doing the job wrong.

At this date it does indeed seem that Randall's theatre is falling flat on at least its critical face: its first two shows were panned by both the *Times* and *The New Yorker*. None of the reviewers I read wrote, as Sobel had hoped they would, that the classics require more work than they got in Randall's productions, though Mimi Kramer in *The New Yorker* did observe that Randall was using "celebrities not particularly known for their stage acting" in shows "empty of any of the underused first-rate stage actors one sees just in New York." Nor did anyone I read note that the Pearl was already doing an annual season of classics with a resident company. The *Times*, in fact, ran a piece on other attempts like

Randall's under the head: "Wanted (Still): A Home for the Classics." The piece listed nine companies, the first dating from 1763. It listed neither the Pearl nor the Jean Cocteau, which also stages classics every season. A paranoid might conclude that there was a conspiracy of silence designed to give Randall's six million a clear field. Perhaps; but plain sloppiness seems to me a likelier explanation. Conspiracy requires tight editing.

◯ JANUARY 7

Frank Geraci is facing me across the big desk in his apartment this afternoon when he tells me he has tested HIV-positive.

AIDS is striking the small world of the Pearl for the second time this season. In September Ivan Polley, the fund-raiser, died at thirty-four, and now I learn that its precursor, HIV (human immunodeficiency virus), afflicts the company's senior male member.

"I tested positive a year and a half ago, on my fiftieth birthday. Given my life-style for the past twenty years, I wasn't surprised." There's a hint of that life-style in the poster on Geraci's wall for the Saint, a gay disco of the 1980s. "I thought I could handle it," he says. His voice is firm and calm; this small, graying man sitting very still and alone at his desk seems fully in control of himself. He continues: "I've seen people die in front of me. I've dealt with people with AIDS [Geraci objects vigorously when I refer to them as "victims"]. I've had an ex-lover who staged his own demise. I've had a dear, dear friend who died during rehearsal. I had to clean out his apartment for three days. I can count probably on one hand the friends I have left in New York.

"I've been very fortunate to be with a doctor who got me into a New York Hospital study. I've been following their treatment for a year and a half, but I haven't the faintest idea if it's helping or not. Every month they test me, take my blood. They get my T-cell count—T cells help regulate virus. A healthy count is about one thousand, and anytime you get below five hundred you're in trouble. Mine is steadily going down. It's now eighty-six. But I don't feel the difference."

I observe that he seems to me in excellent condition. "I feel the same physically as I did before the test," Geraci says. "The only difference is that it's made me less patient." After a moment he says: "Nobody knows. There's lots of factors involved. One is, you have to have a plan, you need some sort of goal, something ahead, something to create. I have lots of energy. I need to put this energy into something concrete.

"I've been doing a lot of writing," he tells me. He gets up to go to a bookcase and brings to the desk five big loose-leaf notebooks that he says contain diaries he's been keeping for twenty years. He's going over his diaries as part of "putting order into this life."

Earlier that afternoon Geraci told me about his "Seattle dream." "I'm fifty-two, I've gotta make a move," he said. He felt he had to leave the Pearl after eight years. "Shep and I have given each other ample reason to part company. I can't even listen to him direct anymore because he's too constrictive, too much 'Don't do this,' 'Don't do that.' *Tartuffe* was the last straw." Seattle was where Geraci could do what he really wanted: "I've reached the point in my life where I want to direct, I want to have my own company, have more say in casting." He also wanted to act in a movie, and he has close friends in Seattle who are filmmakers. He said he intended to leave in a couple of months. "I won't be back," he said. "I don't see myself driving a cab in New York."

Now, after telling me he has tested positive, Geraci says: "I might have to change a lot of plans if I start waking up with cold sweats. We always hear that's the first sign [that the virus has advanced to AIDS itself]."

In the present Geraci finds a refuge in various kinds of exercise: he is very much aware of the body that is such an essential part of the actor's instrument. "I've found something in snorkel-ing," he says, and when I look surprised he explains that he uses the snorkel to keep his face underwater while swimming laps in a pool. "It's incredible, it's prenatal," he says enthusiastically. "It's the only exercise I've ever done where I can go past exhaus-tion. I can hear my body as I never could. I don't get upset stomachs anymore. I never looked so good in my life." More slowly he says: "I don't know how long it's going to last. . . ." His voice trails off and he turns to look out the window.

Finally he says, still gazing out the window: "I'm not talking about a cure, but about a way to live each day."

JANUARY 10

Laura Rathgeb and I are talking about her performance as Cassandra in *The Trojan Women,* which ended its run a month ago.

Rathgeb doesn't want to tell me the year of her birth—"I've been advised not to, because of casting"—but she does say she's still under thirty, though barely. That makes her the junior member of the Pearl company, and she's able to assume a much younger manner, which served her well a few years back as Puck in *A Midsummer Night's Dream.* She's a strong-boned, sturdy young woman, with large brown eyes in a round face set in a mane of thick brown hair. To me her features suggest a Slavic origin; in fact, her background is German and Irish, and she says her high school Latin teacher told her she looked Etruscan.

Of all the actors I've met this season, Rathgeb is the only one who comes from a theatre family. Her parents run St. Michael's Playhouse in Colchester, Vermont, where Rathgeb spends her summers as assistant producer and actress. She was always headed for an acting career. She explains the attraction of performing before a live audience by quoting a fragment from a prayer to the patron saint of actors, Saint Genesius: "This talent you have granted us, the power to sway the thoughts and feelings of others with our acting . . ." She says she would recite that prayer with her parents.

Acting also offers other identities into which Rathgeb can escape from the shyness to which she freely confesses. She's always seemed uncomfortable with me, her conversation very serious but punctuated by occasional nervous laughter. The other actors have all talked easily with me. They've accepted and have even seemed to welcome my inquiring presence as long as I obeyed theatre protocol (such as staying away from them in the hour before a performance). "It's good to have you here asking all these questions," Robin Leslie Brown once told me. "It makes us think about what we're doing." Yet they haven't solicited my ear. It's been almost a year now, and never has one of the actors phoned me except to return my call. It occurs to me that if I were dealing with the usual fare of political and financial connivers, my telephone line would be swamped.

Though she's uneasy while we talk, Rathgeb wanted this conversation about Cassandra. It is an exceptionally difficult role. Like all the Trojan women, she is doomed to a tragic fate, and she is also to some degree demented. Cassandra is a priestess who was given as a bride to Apollo. She can foresee the future but no one will believe her predictions. When she appears she is about to be taken away by the Greek Agamemnon as a concubine. She comes on stage weirdly laughing and dancing. (Rathgeb's movements were created by Alice Tierstein, Sobel's choreographer cousin.) Cassandra asks her sorrowing mother, Hecuba, to join her in celebrating her wedding to their conqueror because in that future only she can see the Greeks' fate will be even worse than that of the Trojans and she herself will murder Agamemnon.

"I don't know any way to do Cassandra without going to some pretty scary places inside me," Rathgeb says. She quotes director Anthony Cornish as saying that the Greeks wrote only the third

Above, in Euripides' great tragedy The Trojan Women, *Bella Jarrett as Hecuba, widow of King Priam of Troy—a role so demanding that it has been called "King Lear for women." Below, the three members of the chorus are played by (from left) Diane Paulus, Joanne Camp, and Belynda Fay Hardin.*

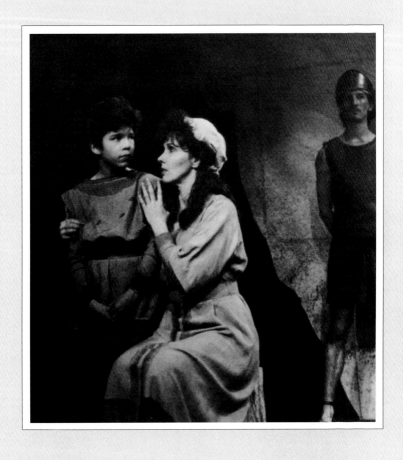

Above, Andromache, widow of Hector—played by Donnah Welby, a member of the Pearl company—holds their son moments before the triumphant Greeks take the boy away to be killed. The boy is played by Carlo Alban, and the Greek soldier at right by Hank Wagner, the Pearl's acting apprentice. Opposite top, Helen of Troy, played by Robin Leslie Brown, pleads for her life with Menelaus, the Greek husband she abandoned for the Trojan prince Paris. Menelaus is played by Stuart Lerch. Opposite bottom, Laura Rathgeb as Cassandra.

Rosalind, in As You Like It, *is one of Shakespeare's greatest roles and a favorite of Joanne Camp, who is playing it for the third time. With her is Arnie Burton, as Orlando. Below, Joanne Camp's Rosalind with Phebe, played by Donnah Welby.*

acts of their plays. To Rathgeb, that means she must relive what happens to Cassandra before the play begins—the first two acts of her story—and then find the courage to come on stage and face her fate at the hands of the Greeks. "I had to spend an incredible time preparing," she says. "I had to go through really horrible things that happen to Cassandra in those first two acts. I imagined being raped by Ajax—remember, I'm a virgin priestess—and I imagined them killing my father [King Priam]. To heighten it, I would imagine that the Greeks ripped him from my arms and my mother and I had to watch while they stabbed him to death." Here the young woman's voice quivers as she once more imagines her own parents suffering the fate of the Trojans. "I had to avoid thinking about my own mother too much or I'd have made a mess of myself."

She waits a moment before going on. "The scariest time was what I had to face on stage. I had to marry this man [Agamemnon] that I imagined as the embodiment of the devil. Then one night about two weeks into the run I had a nightmare in which I actually went to bed with that devil, with his beady red eyes and his ugly evil face." She laughs uneasily at the memory: it was the kind of nightmare that stays with us for months or forever. "When I start dreaming my role I know it's gotten into my subconscious."

Rathgeb shakes off the nightmare and her voice changes as she turns to religion and faith: Cassandra's and her own. "It was interesting walking around as a pagan for a few months," says this believing Christian. "You know, you find elements of doubt in the gods in Euripides. I let that reverberate in me. Cassandra and I both have doubted our faith. She had to see the Greeks kill her father on the altar of Zeus. Where were the gods then? I would think of Christ's words on the cross: 'My God, my God, why hast thou forsaken me?' "

⌇ JANUARY 15

Good news: the Pearl's new fund-raiser, Larry Auld, calls to tell me an unexpected check for $10,000 from a foundation has arrived in the morning mail. That, plus the two best weeks of the season at the box office, takes the bank account out of its immediate danger, though it does not guarantee a successful end to the season, and still less does it assure that the Pearl can afford to stay on Off Broadway next year. But Mary Harpster can pay all the bills: in the makeshift financial world of small theatres, that's stability. And it should get better before it gets worse.

When *As You Like It* ends its run in just under two weeks, the Pearl's bank account will benefit in two more ways. The payroll for actors will drop from fourteen to five (the number of actors in *Ghosts*, the next play), a weekly saving of $1,620. The Pearl will also be getting a refund of money now on deposit with Actors' Equity. Knowing how suddenly theatres can vanish, leaving their players unpaid, Equity requires the theatres to deposit two weeks' salary per actor as guaranteed severance pay. With the smaller cast of *Ghosts*, the Pearl's deposit will drop by $3,240.

As You Like It is selling out or close to it at every performance. That's been true since the production got a favorable notice from Mel Gussow, the *New York Times*'s chief Off Broadway reviewer. Gussow's review, though by far the most important at the box office, is only one of eight. That's more attention in print than the Pearl has ever gotten, and all eight reviewers liked most of what they saw. All of them praised Joanne Camp's Rosalind, and a couple noted that Stuart Lerch's Jaques gave his famous speech without sounding like an actor giving a famous speech. Lerch spoke the lines as he told me he would: as if Shakespeare had written them just for him. Most satisfyingly, many of the writers commented that the production achieved two of Sobel's major goals for the Pearl: clarity of speech—Shakespeare that you can actually understand!—and fidelity to the author. One reviewer commended the Pearl for doing what Shaw advised in his 1896 review of a production of *As You Like It:* "For years we have been urging the managers to give us Shakespeare's plays as he wrote them, playing them intelligently and enjoyingly as pleasant stories, instead of mutilating them, altering them, and celebrating them as superstitious rites."

It strikes me as ironic that the fidelity to the author that everyone is lauding today is the same fidelity that reviewers were complaining about in the Pearl's two earlier productions. No one is asking for a Wall Street Rosalind or a Shakespeare that gives a "nod to the twentieth century," as one writer wanted from *Tartuffe.* There's an authoritarian undertone to the idea of making modern adaptations of the classics. If you set *The Trojan Women* in this century you are inevitably narrowing the spectators' responses to those you—not Euripides—have chosen for them. You'll have to pick a war and some villainous victors in place of the Greeks, and those choices will carry contemporary political freight about which the author has no say. Those who want the modern implications of the classics spelled out aren't so much worried that we won't get the author's point as they are that we won't get *their* point.

I've learned that I needn't have worried that people would find unconvincing Arnie Burton's victory in his wrestling match with the much bigger and more muscular Alex Leydenfrost. One reviewer praised the fight scene for its effectiveness and reported he'd heard a "collective gasp." The night we attended, Janice did indeed gasp when Leydenfrost's mouth filled with what seemed to be blood after a particularly heavy blow from Burton. We were in the fourth row, and I wondered if the actors could hear that gasp. When I told Sobel this, he laughed and said: "I hope so. Then they'll know they're doing it right." He also said

Leydenfrost was falling so realistically that the impact of his 215 pounds had so weakened the underpinnings of the stage that they'd had to be repaired.

(At intermission that night I encountered another example of what a lack of money does to Pearl-sized theatres. Bill McComb, the affable young stage manager, told me before he climbed the ladder to the light booth that he was leaving to work on a musical called *1492* in North Carolina. In two weeks there, he said, he'd earn as much as the Pearl would pay him for the eleven weeks of *As You Like It*. "I love the Pearl," he said somewhat apologetically, one foot on the bottom rung of the ladder. "But I don't feel guilty, because I'm leaving the show in good shape." Still, stage managers for two of the first three shows have broken their contracts—legitimately, by Equity's rules—to take better-paying jobs elsewhere.)

People at the Pearl are smiling these days, but no one is smiling as much as Joanne Camp. "I'm just in heaven," she tells me that afternoon when I catch up with her in the women's dressing room. "I haven't had this much fun as an actor since heaven knows when. I wasn't an actor when I did Rosalind before. I'm more of an actor now." With less than two weeks to go, the show is still changing in small ways: "She's a slightly different person every night." Camp's exploration of Rosalind is never-ending. "There are still places where I'd like to understand her a little better," she says. I ask about her goals for the remainder of the run. Her tone is emphatic: "I'd like to feel every moment true, and Rosalind all one person, not divided between Rosalind and Joanne. I like it when Rosalind takes over and she makes the choices. Joanne's instinctive reactions become those of Rosalind. It's hard because Shakespeare requires so much technique to handle the language, if you get carried away you may lose the audience. But if everything's perfectly married it can work. Rosalind can only speak with the clarity you need because that's the way she naturally speaks." Her big green eyes are sparkling. "It's incredibly exciting. It's the ultimate thrill of acting."

"For one thing, she's stopped worrying about her age and talking about that face-lift," her husband says good-humoredly when I ask him what it's like to live with Joanne Camp while she's playing the role she's dreamed of for almost ten years. "She has lots more energy. She's doing exercises and eating healthy." The difference is evident at the very beginning of their day: "Joanne seldom wakes up before I do—except when she's playing Rosalind."

✿ JANUARY 25

Sobel and I and a bucket of leek-and-potato soup are rattling up the West Side in a borrowed car. The soup is our household's contribution to feeding the Pearl's actors tomorrow night, between the last two performances of *As You Like It*. While he pilots us skillfully among the potholes, and I clutch our soup bucket, Sobel is talking about the next show, Ibsen's *Ghosts*, now in its next-to-last week of rehearsal.

Ibsen's sombre play is as wrenching a change from Shakespeare's enchanted Forest of Arden as the tragedy of *The Trojan Women* was from the biting comedy of Moliere's *Tartuffe*. The title refers to the habits of conforming to social hypocrisy that the protagonist, Mrs. Alving, has to exorcise in order to find her true self. The play was a shocker in its day, so much so that its first production was not in Ibsen's Norway but in Chicago, in 1882. Dale Ramsey, the Pearl's dramaturge, recalled that the censor of the Copenhagen Royal Theatre said of *Ghosts:* "It takes as the main theme of its action a repulsive pathological phenomenon, at the same time undermining the morality which forms the foundation of our social order." Other than that, it was presumably acceptable.

The "pathological phenomenon" was a disease that could not

be named in public in Ibsen's day and for generations there-after—syphilis. One day in rehearsal I listened to the director, Robert Brink, and the five actors discussing the disease. They spoke of syphilis as something out of history, like leprosy. I was reminded that they are all considerably younger than I, and that syphilis, though in fact thriving, is no longer the major social reality to most Americans that it once was. I wondered in passing if I was the only person present who had undergone a Wasser-mann test.

That same day, during a break in rehearsal, I got another lesson in the harsh financial facts of life in live theatre. I was talking with Michael Levin, the veteran actor who plays the major role of the hypocritical Pastor Manders. Levin is the rare actor who has combined a career in serious theatre with one in soap opera, where he was known as Jack Fenelli in "Ryan's Hope." During the break he told me that on the coming Mon-day, their day off, he was going to film two episodes in another soap, "As the World Turns." He was to play a patient in a coma. He was called for two o'clock and expected to be in the studio coma bed less than two hours. His acting would consist of wig-gling his finger, twice. For that wiggled finger Levin would earn more than he would for the entire eleven weeks of *Ghosts*.

Sobel has been unhappy with Robert Brink's directing since the early rehearsals. "We're being asked to watch people having emotions, instead of pursuing actions," he says in the car. "For an actor, the emotion is homework, it's there to serve the action. After all, this is called acting, not emoting." For the last two weeks Sobel has been making his objections known in the record of meetings with the director:

January 13, 1992, in response to run-through of act I: "It needs a lot of picking up in color, pace, mood, everything.

"Manders . . . is very slow, not only of pace but, it would seem, of mind. The audience is way ahead of him. I'm afraid we're seeing some soap-opera habits.

"Generally:

"Talk to each other, and find actions to pursue, never moods to play.

"Select what's important in a speech and scene; everything cannot be of the same import and weight.

"Lighten up; speed up.

"Turn this act over to the actors now. They're ready to shift away from the guiding hand of the director [referring to Brink's habit of standing close to the actors on stage rather than directing them from offstage]."

On January 17, 1992, in response to the run-through of act II: "Mrs A. [Alving] is now receiving and digesting; can she get to acting and pursuing purpose." Again on Mrs. Alving, on the morning of the day we are traveling uptown together: "She's playing meaning, not a person yet. And it must be hers, not director's."

Now, as we make our way up Sixth Avenue, Sobel makes it clear he is still unhappy with the show: "It's still terribly slow. It moves like a soap opera. People digest their emotions on stage instead of expressing them. We've got to cut fifteen minutes! Bob Brink says he agrees, but I don't know if he really does or he's just saying it to put me off." Sobel is as pessimistic as Ibsen himself. Time is running out. "Next week is our last chance to fix it."

JANUARY 25–26

We're sitting in a ragged circle on the stage floor around a spread of food: three Crockpots of soup, bread, cheese, and salad. It's about eight o'clock on Saturday night, and the cast is eating between the five and nine o'clock shows of *As You Like It*. Under Equity rules, the theatre is required to supply a meal when, as is the case with this longest play of the season, the cast has less than ninety minutes between performances. The Pearl sent out a call for food donations, and we are eating the typically mixed-up results. It's the last night of the run, and the mood among the actors is one of both pleasure and regret. The play is a joyous one to perform, it's been a critical and box office success, and the actors—about half-and-half resident company and jobbers new to the Pearl—have gotten along exceptionally well.

A rich chocolate cake is brought on stage to mark the occasion. It's inscribed "Love and Thanks—Tony" and is from Anthony Cornish, who is now directing a show in Florida. The cast applauds their director's sweet remembrance and one actor says, "I quite like the idea that we're having this cake," in imitation of a standard Cornish expression. Sobel now enters our circle to announce major good news. The Barter Theatre in Abingdon, Virginia, has invited the Pearl production to come there in June. The actors all clap and cheer, and with reason: this means six weeks of work at relatively good pay ($424 a week compared to the Pearl's $180). With his usual thoughtfulness, Sobel is careful to credit his good tidings to Frank Lowe, one of the jobbers, who suggested the idea to the artistic director at the Barter.

Joanne Camp heard the news that afternoon. It meant far more to her than to the other actors. Always moody, Camp had been in a blue funk for the past week. In the morning she'd snapped angrily for no reason at someone she met in a store. No reason, except that the biggest role of her career was drawing to its close. She and Rosalind were about to part, this time forever. Never again would she inhabit Rosalind's heart and mind and body. "I came for the five o'clock show and I went in the men's dressing room," she told me later. "Arnie [Burton] took one look, he hugged me, and we were both crying. Tonight's the last time for Rosalind, I said to him, because now I'm really too old for her. Then Shep came in and told us about the Barter Theatre." I asked about her immediate response to the news. "I put my head in my hands on the dressing-room table and I said: 'There is a God! After all, there is a God!'"

The nine o'clock show plays to an enthusiastic full house. (I watch it from the light booth above the last row.) The cast dances their curtain calls in a joyful circle, and then it's all over. A few minutes later the actors, out of costume, are embracing each other and saying their farewells. Camp is in the lobby surrounded by friends and fans. She takes a moment to tell me about the last performance: "In our last scene Dan [Daily] and I both were crying. Dan can't go to Virginia, so for him it really was the last time." She shakes her head in exasperation, and now I see the fanatical edge on her dedication to her demanding profession: "It's so unprofessional for an actor to cry on stage like that. It's unfair to the audience." Then she turns away to bestow her dazzling smile on still another well-wisher.

Sobel meanwhile is already at work on the next job: to dismantle this set to make way for the next. It's a job that will go on into the small hours of the night and resume early tomorrow morning. Snow starts falling while I am walking home.

Next morning a dozen people are working on the stage. They are literally deconstructing Shakespeare's Forest of Arden. The set consists of vines made of intertwined artificial leaves and flowers that hang down at the back of the stage. Sobel, standing on the balcony, detaches the vines and tosses them to the stage, where someone—staff or volunteer—coils each carefully and puts it in a box for possible use in the Virginia production in June. In place of Shakespeare's light and dreamlike forest will go the heavy wood and dark colors of a nineteenth-century Norwegian living room. This is where the grim drama of Ibsen's *Ghosts* will run its appointed course. Soon the volunteers turn from coiling vines to painting Ibsen's interior.

Janice and I are assigned to the task of untangling floral decorations in the lobby. We're removing the decorative strands from the lobby walls and then detaching the flowers and leaves and sorting them into boxes where they will await another show. While we work we are chatting with Colleen Davis, the Pearl's apprentice stage manager, who turned twenty-two on the opening day of *The Trojan Women.* Davis's black hair and hazel eyes, and her cheerful disposition, all live up to her Irish name. In her junior year at Lehigh University Davis discovered her calling was theatre, not mathematics, her then major. "A lot of people in my class were looking for careers, thinking about buying homes and cars, dreaming of being the next Lee Iacocca. That bothered me. I couldn't figure out why till I started hanging out with people who just wanted to be happy. That's what they wanted out of life. In college, stage managing was what made me happy." Although she'd acted in a couple of shows she never gave serious thought to pursuing an acting career: she knew she was destined for the ground crew.

Davis's face still has some of the unformed look of a teenager, but in fact she is being rapidly shaped by her experience at the Pearl. She works a different job with each show. For *Tartuffe* she was up in the booth operating the lights, and then she ran Donna Riley's complex sound design for *The Trojan Women.* She worked the box office for *As You Like It.* Along with these duties she's assisted the stage manager. She's prompted the actors, which means following the text during rehearsal so closely that she can respond without pause to the actor's cry of "Line!" She's given line notes, which also requires her to follow the text closely. Starting late in the rehearsal period, she notes the errors each actor makes and reports them in a note she puts in the actor's mailbox. The purpose is to prevent the errors from getting firmly entrenched in the actor's memory. "It's a job nobody likes," she says.

Davis is also learning to survive in the big city, no easy accomplishment for a rather vulnerable-looking young woman from rural New Jersey, who now goes home to a New York apartment alone late at night on the subway. I ask her about the nightly trip home. "I live in a neat neighborhood," she says enthusiastically. She's apartment-sitting on East Ninety-ninth Street, the only way she can get by on the $75 a week the Pearl pays her. "The old men who play dominoes on the street wouldn't let anyone bother me. Also I have my favorite homeless person. He's a young black guy named Craig who gives me copies of the *New York Times* he finds and walks me home at night. He hangs out around the subway stop. I let him walk me to my block but not to my door. I met him one day outside the Laundromat when I was waiting for my laundry. We started chatting. He keeps asking me for money but I never give him any. 'I work in the theatre and you're asking me for money?' I say to him. He still follows me around because I laugh at his jokes."

In five years—Davis says in answer to a question—"I'd like to be earning enough to pay my rent, to eat and to travel, and to see all the shows I want." A modest goal for a graduate in business administration but not so easy in the theatre: after many more years than five, none of the Pearl actors has met that standard. That, in any case, is not what really matters to her: "I want to have a reputation, to be a me. I want to be known to be good. When a director has an especially difficult show that needs a very good stage manager—I want people to say: 'Get Colleen Davis!' "

I wander off in search of Joanne Camp and find her sitting at her desk in the upstairs office. She's back in her familiar and decidedly un-Shakespearean jeans. She is leafing through a huge pile of photos and résumés sent in by actors or their agents in hope of an audition. This is part of Camp's second job as the Pearl's casting director. Despite the name, the casting director does not cast. She selects the actors to audition for the artistic director—Sobel—who will cast them, usually after a second audition.

The Pearl holds two kinds of auditions, Camp explains, auditions for an announced role and general auditions in which Sobel is just getting acquainted with an actor he may want to call for sometime later on. "For the role of a young man or a young woman, we may get as many as five hundred of these," Camp says, indicating the pile of photos and résumés. Poor odds, but better than the general auditions which the Pearl holds every spring. Each actor gets five minutes to do two monologues. Sobel and Camp will hear eleven actors an hour, four hours a day, for a total of about two hundred. "Many actors come unprepared," Camp says, disgust in her voice. "They barely know their lines. They kill their own chances!" At best, those chances aren't very good. Still, the Pearl gets most of its understudies this way, and Kathryn Lee, who played Mariane in *Tartuffe*, came to Camp's attention at a general audition.

It's evident that Camp is once more in a gloomy mood. The radiance of Rosalind is gone from those big green eyes. The emotional seesaw on which she lives, down yesterday morning, lifted sky-high last night by the news she could play Rosalind one more time, is back down on the ground. I ask her what's wrong. She shrugs. "I'm looking for work and it's so depressing," she says. "I've played Broadway, I've just successfully done one of Shakespeare's most important roles—and still I have to go out and try to sell myself to strangers and be rejected. I'm writing to the casting directors of soap operas asking for work as a day player [one-shot appearances that pay the actor $700 a day]." She shakes her head, her strawberry-blond hair flying, and, as angry at herself as she is at the world, she says: "And I blew an audition last week! It was for a part on Broadway, in the American cast of *Dancing at Lughnasa* [an Irish play whose original cast was going home]. I auditioned for one role and I was called back, but for another role. I played it strong when the character should be weak. I just blew it."

She pauses, then continues in a reflective tone: "It does something to you. You start downgrading yourself. You tell yourself, the only reason you did Rosalind well is because it's the third time and by now of course you can do it. It's frightening. It's dangerous." Camp falls silent. After a moment she returns to the immediate task of sorting through the pile of would-be entrants into this profession, young people who would love nothing better than to risk the anguish she's suffering today in return for a chance, no matter how remote, to experience what the same Joanne Camp two weeks ago was calling "the ultimate thrill of acting."

〰 MARCH 6

In Chekhov's *Swan Song* an old actor at the end of his career is musing over his stage life. For Claude Underwood the role proved to be indeed his swan song.

It happened halfway through the second of only three weeks of rehearsal for the four one-act comedies the Pearl is to present under the title *Chekhov Very Funny*. Sobel's idea in putting on the one-acters was to rescue Chekhov from the slow and mournful style in which he is too often played. He cut the rehearsal time by a week to save his own time—he is directing because he couldn't find anyone he liked for the job—and because he thought the three farces that accompany *Swan Song* might lose their freshness if overrehearsed.

As Sobel recounted it to me by telephone a week later, Claude Underwood was an actor in his mid-sixties who was delighted to be back on stage after an absence of several years. It was his first time at the Pearl. "You couldn't believe his glee when he was cast," Sobel said. "He was so happy, it was almost unnatural. He rushed over for the script, he was in a bit of a panic over the lines. He was a sweet, enthusiastic man, and he needed to calm down. It worried me that he was so nervous during the first rehearsal. He realized he was working at a level he wasn't used to. He'd been doing class B and he felt this was class A. He did settle down after the first day, and then last Wednesday he was in the middle of his Hamlet speech when he said: 'I've got to stop a minute. I'm having trouble breathing.' We waited, but it didn't go away, and after three or four minutes Dan said: 'I don't want to push the panic button, but does it feel like a weight on your chest?' [Dan Daily, who played the two dukes in *As You Like It*, is back to play four roles in the Chekhovs.] 'Sort of,' Claude said, and at that everyone stood up. The stage manager got out the medical sheet listing allergies and emergency contacts that she keeps on each actor, I went to the phone and called Bruce Yaffe [a physician who is a Pearl trustee]. We got Claude to the phone—it wasn't an easy trip for him—and he talked to Bruce. Bruce advised Claude to go for an EKG at Lenox Hill Hospital. Colleen [Davis] and I took him to Lenox Hill, which is on the Upper East Side. It was the longest cab ride ever. The hospital people were singularly unhelpful, but we finally got Claude to the emergency room. I left Colleen there and told her to call in every hour. I came back here to rehearse an understudy who was going on that night in *Ghosts*."

Sobel interrupted his account to take another call, then resumed: "We were told that night Claude had had a small heart attack on stage. I began thinking about how to replace him when they said he'd be out at least four or five days. Then when I called the next morning—that was Thursday—they told me he was having open-heart surgery. My God, I thought. They said he'd had a ruptured aorta in the hospital. Claude died that night." Sobel was silent for a long moment. "There's no thought that we killed him," he said slowly. "But he wanted it too much. He wanted it so much it was bad for his health."

Colleen Davis, the apprentice stage manager, would later recall the event as a maturing experience. She'd never held anything approaching the responsibility Sobel assigned her by leaving her alone in the hospital that day. It was the second brush with mortality this season—Ivan Polley's death from AIDS was the other—for a young woman who'd had little to do with death. "In college everyone's eighteen to twenty-two and nobody dies," she told me.

"Frank Geraci," Sobel said, to my surprise, when I asked him who was replacing Underwood. "I thought he was going to Seattle," I said, remembering the plan Geraci had outlined to me not long ago to move out there and leave New York and the Pearl and Sobel forever. Sobel laughed and said: "Frank's been threatening me with Seattle for years. I don't think there *is* a Seattle!"

When I spoke to Geraci backstage during a break in the rehearsal of *Swan Song*—*his* swan song now—it was the first time I'd seen him since the day two months earlier when he told me he'd tested HIV-positive. The short, graying actor looked as healthy as he always had; if his plans were changed, his manner was not. I asked why he'd come back to a show directed by Sobel after their falling-out during *Tartuffe*. "It was only ten days to the first preview, and I knew the material," Geraci said. "A large part of me was happy I could help save the day." I said that didn't seem enough of an explanation. He smiled almost apologetically and said: "I can't leave. It's because of my health. I have to work. I have to act. That's where my energy comes from." So, he said, he was trying to repair his working relationship with Sobel, and he thought Sobel was meeting him halfway. "With only ten days to go, we both had to buckle down and not indulge our personal problems with each other."

Rather than go to Seattle—though he intends to go there someday—Geraci said he'd decided to put on a one-man show of his own. "I'd had it in the back of my mind," he said. "Then one day I said to Shep: 'A lot of my criticism of your directing derives from my need to direct.' And Shep said: 'Why don't you direct something?' When I was walking home that night I decided I'd do it, and I'd do the whole thing myself. So I'll be my own director and my own producer." Geraci will present the show at the Pearl in late April and early May.

"Doing two shows at the same time doesn't leave much time for despair," he said when I asked about his spirits. Would he be doing the show if he hadn't tested positive? "That's a good question," he said, and after a long pause: "Probably not. No, surely not. HIV gave me the drive to take care of things now— not that I think it's all over. It gave me my first real sense of mortality."

🐦 MARCH 14

Surprisingly, *Ghosts* has turned out to be a hit.

When it closes tonight, Ibsen's grim tale will have run at 91 percent of capacity and brought in $35,408 at the box office. That record matches the previous show, *As You Like It*, which was expected to be the season's best seller, and it exceeds *Tartuffe* (which played to 82 percent of capacity) and *The Trojan Women* (70 percent).

The reviews have been both favorable and plentiful. Among the eight publications that commented on *Ghosts* are the *Norway Times*, which contented itself with quoting its New York namesake, and, oddly, a Hebrew-language paper. Jerry Tallmer, in the New York *Post*, even wrote that in recent years *Ghosts* has become *more* timely:

> Everything comes to a climax in a famous overwrought scene of clutching and crying between Oswald and his mama . . . with Oswald begging his mother to feed him the morphine that will end his agony and his existence. Overwrought? Yes, I once thought so, but that was a few years ago when I was young and stupid and people were not begging their husbands, or their wives, or their lovers, or their children, to disconnect the machinery, or to connect the fatal machinery. And once I thought, and wrote, that *Ghosts* was passé because syphilis had been effectively wiped from the planet—but that was 25 years ago, and then along came something called AIDS.

At the last hour, director Robert Brink picked up the slow pace that was still troubling Sobel on the eve of the opening. Gone is the turgid soap-opera feeling I'd noticed in rehearsal. The night we attended the show no one in our group thought it slow-moving. I noticed Robin Leslie Brown, as Regina, obeying

Sobel's frequent request that the actors pay "constant, physical attention" to what other actors are saying. In a scene where she is silent while two others are talking, Brown's Regina not only listened constantly but by her body language she made me see her listening.

There's one notable exception to this chorus of praise for the Pearl's production—Sobel himself. When we're sitting uncomfortably on straight-backed chairs in the men's dressing room drinking lukewarm coffee, Sobel shakes his head and says: "It's not a great show. Of course I'm glad it sold a lot of tickets and got great reviews. Still, it's a downer to stand out there in the lobby and listen to compliments about a show that I know wasn't doing what it could do." At first I suspect Sobel is tasting sour grapes because public and reviewers are embracing a show whose direction he dislikes after they shunned and panned—relatively, anyway—the two earlier shows he himself directed. But as he goes on, I see more clearly than I ever have the lofty target at which Sobel wants his theatre to aim: "People come out of *Ghosts* very impressed by the production and the acting. 'She must have been so upset,' they say. 'Did you hear that scream?' " Sobel leans forward in his chair and his voice rises to underline his words: "It doesn't matter if she's upset. It matters if the audience is upset. It matters if the audience is living the experience. That's the purpose of art, to enable us to live the experience without actually paying the physical price. You can't understand experience in any deep sense without living it."

It's true, I realize, that after the show our group talked much more about the performances than about the story. By that criterion we were indeed more impressed than moved.

"Art shouldn't ask for an intellectual response. The response we're getting to *Ghosts* doesn't compare to a man I remember who came out of the theatre one night wanting to compliment us on our production, but he couldn't say it. He was too moved to get the words out. So he gave up on the compliment—and he went off with the show."

❧ MARCH 16

This morning brings the most startling news of the season: Sobel is firing Donnah Welby.

The beautiful, dark-haired Welby has been at the Pearl since the beginning and is, or so it seems to me, a great asset to the company. The Pearl has no stars, but if it did, she'd surely be one. She's played many important roles. Her Andromache in *The Trojan Women* earlier this season was well received by audiences and critics, and for me was an emotional high point of the year. Her playful, witty presence was one of the pleasures of being around the Pearl.

Sobel's manner as he tells me that he is dropping from the company both Welby and Laura Rathgeb, the youngest member, who is in her fifth season, is noticeably different from his usual breezy style. Sobel in my experience always knows what he wants to say, but usually he makes sure his manner of saying it is informal. Today he sounds like a man reading a prepared statement. "Laura is on a sabbatical of undetermined length," he says. "Donnah's membership is not being renewed." He emphasizes, still speaking in carefully chosen words, that the decision was his alone.

Each spring Sobel offers—or does not offer—the actors membership in the company for the coming season. Usually it happens at the end of the annual private meeting Sobel has with each member. They discuss the actor's work during the season. Sobel's comments, and the actors' responses, are recorded on a form that is supposed to be seen by no one except the two of them. In this case, however, Sobel notified Welby and Rathgeb well in advance so they could make other plans for next year.

By Sobel's account the tone of the two meetings was very

different. About Rathgeb he says: "We had a long talk and eventually I think we came to an understanding. At the Pearl she works under stress. It's difficult for her to make the transition from being a junior member. She always feels judged, as if she were an intern. She needs experience elsewhere to have confidence in her work. I hope she'll be back."

But about Welby he says: "We had a short meeting, we didn't agree, and I told her I wasn't going to renew her membership. I find it hard to work with Donnah. I'm not satisfied with her approach to her work. Her performance is always satisfactory, always pleasing to the audience. But she won't take risks. She doesn't want to be what I want every actor in the company to want to be. Donnah's content to be a good actress. She doesn't want to try to be a great one." Now, as I listen, I recall that I'd seen some warning signals. I'd been surprised, for instance, when, in response to my praise of Welby's Andromache, Sobel had said that "Euripides had something to do with it." For Sobel, the remark seemed far out of character; I wondered if he would have said anything like that about other actors in the company. I knew, too, that he'd passed Welby over for two major roles this season, Dorine in *Tartuffe* and Mrs. Alving in *Ghosts*. The two roles got excellent performances from outside actors who probably would not have been willing to play the Pearl under its old Off Off Broadway contract.

Donnah Welby's voice at the other end of the line is furious. She recalls a hasty, angry meeting at a coffee shop near her Times Square office: "Shep was looking at his feet when he told me I wasn't being invited back. I said to him, 'This sucks. I've put in eight years. I've done great work for you, I've gotten great reviews.' He used us actors for cheap labor when he was building the company and now he's trying to get rid of us. We built that theatre! We put in the sets, we put in the seats. I used to make my own costumes." Welby recalls with a bitter laugh the end of their exchange in the coffee shop: "He left in such a hurry he didn't even pay for his goddam coffee!" When I ask her if she is content to be good rather than great she turns the question back on Sobel: "What great actress is going to work for a hundred and eighty fucking dollars a week? He wants great acting but he isn't willing to pay for it. He wants me to work another job for forty hours a week so I can afford to act at the Pearl."

Welby says she believes she was fired because of Joanne Camp: "I got along with everyone except his wife. Joanne ganged up on me. She tried to turn everyone against me. Joanne's gotten rid of most people there—now there's only two left of the original twenty-two in the company." That there was ill feeling between the two does not come as a surprise to me. From the first, I'd had a sense of rivalry about them, and it seemed to me that the Pearl's stage must be too small for two such talented and beautiful and strong-willed women. I had noticed also that in my many hours of conversation with Welby and Camp, each avoided talking about the other.

All this lends more than a little irony to some of the Pearl's recent publicity. In my files I find a flier from last fall that includes a photo of Welby and Camp in a half embrace, and a press photo for *As You Like It* that shows them gazing lovingly at each other. But they are both professionals: when watching them on stage together, you would never guess at the antagonism between them.

Camp, whose account of the affair is punctuated with tears, describes a close friendship abruptly ended when, three seasons ago, she criticized Welby's work during a rehearsal of *A Midsummer Night's Dream*. "I said she was holding the play back. I never did it to hurt her, but Donnah never forgave me for that." When I ask about Welby's acting, Camp says: "She can do it if you tell her, but she doesn't ferret it out for herself, and she doesn't work with others." Sobel, however, says that several years ago his wife talked him out of dropping Welby from the company and that he gave Welby some of her best roles on Camp's advice.

Camp concludes her account with: "I'm sick to death of being blamed by people who don't have our commitment." That line brings into sudden focus my picture of what is going on. Sobel and Camp are giving their lives to the Pearl; they are faulting

Welby for not making a similar commitment. Sobel knows he does not and cannot have a company of great actors. What he does ask is that they aspire to greatness. I recall now that he once compared what he wants his actors to do on stage to a photo of an athlete in the act of hurling the javelin. You do not see where the javelin lands; what you do see is the athlete's total commitment to the act of hurling it. I've come to believe that Sobel cares more for becoming than for being. In his concern for the actor's tomorrow, at the occasional expense of today's performance, Sobel is once more the teacher that he was at the start of his career. It is not for nothing—I now realize—that actors occasionally refer to his theatre as "Pearl University."

These are, moreover, people who have worked together for years in an intensely emotional setting. They've been a small band, set apart from most of the world, that devoted their lives to the theatre. Like a couple divorcing, when they part, they will turn some of that intensity against each other: there's no painless way they can separate. Each will blame the other for making the relationship go sour. Beyond the basic issue of commitment, everything they criticize about each other, it now seems to me, is the kind of accumulated grudges and grievances you feed as ammunition to the lawyer handling your divorce. For example, Camp says that Welby "didn't do her job in *The Trojan Women*" and that "Shep's directing gave her almost everything she did." For her part, Welby says she decided during the same show that "Shep's a bad director. I've survived him as long as I could but I can't ever work with him again." Sobel avoids the subject entirely.

(Laura Rathgeb, far more circumspect than Welby in talking to me, nonetheless says: "I feel incredibly used by Shep. I put in a lot of extra work besides acting. Now I'm suddenly thrown away." She says she does not take seriously the idea that she will ever work at the Pearl again. Rathgeb, like Welby, sees Camp at the bottom of her firing. She recalls that a year earlier Sobel told her: "Joanne finds it difficult to accept you as a peer." In fact, Camp says much the same herself. "I haven't always enjoyed working on stage with her," she says. She lists Rathgeb's stage mannerisms that she doesn't like, and adds, clearly not speaking of someone she considers a peer: "I've coached Laura for free and I've found her roles apppropriate for her.")

The issue of Welby's dismissal reaches the Pearl's trustees at their monthly meeting on the evening of the day I hear the news. For the trustees of other theatres, the firing of an actor would be of no more than passing interest; that's art, and their business is business. The Pearl is different. Sobel has made a successful effort to involve the trustees in the life of the theatre. Each board meeting starts with a half hour of what the agenda describes as "artsy stuff": a talk by a director or designer or actor intended to enlighten the board as to what such people do. Trustees and actors and staff mingle at onstage suppers at each gala opening, a custom started by Ken Rotman, president of the board, who would take the whole theatre, fill it with friends, and send out for Chinese food afterwards.

Now that policy is backfiring on Sobel. Ken Rotman says: "Part of the fun of this job is establishing personal relationships with the staff and the company. Now suddenly one of them is gone, after eight years. We not only saw her on stage, we'd come to know her offstage also. It's not a board decision, but we're entitled to know why you did it." Walter Fekula, an investment banker, is particularly upset. Over the years he has become a friend of Welby's as well as an admirer of her work. When he heard of her firing he threatened to quit the board. Sobel's veracity was at issue: he said he'd warned Welby that he wanted a change in her work; Welby said she'd had no warning. The evidence lay in the written record of their annual meetings, but Sobel refused to show Fekula or anyone else these records in order to protect the confidentiality of the meetings. Finally, at Rotman's insistence, he agreed to show Fekula brief excerpts from the records; meanwhile, however, Welby was faxing the entire record to Fekula to sustain *her* version of what happened. It did the opposite: after reading the exchanges between them from 1989 to 1991, Fekula concluded that Sobel had in fact given

Welby due notice that he was dissatisfied; this, not the artistic issue between them, was all that the trustees could concern themselves with. The question of commitment runs through the notes of their conversations. In May 1989 Sobel is saying to Welby: "I am eager to find ways to make you eager. Are you willing to be shaken up, are you willing to be on unsure ground, are you willing not to know anything?" (The last line refers to his belief that Welby relied too much on her earlier training.) The last entry, in April 1991, asks: "The tough choice cannot be delayed: what's your career to be?" Nine months later Welby was telling me much the same when she mused about whether she would take the "leap of faith" and leave her full-time job at the Theatre Development Fund. Sobel spent the hour before the board meeting trying successfully to talk Fekula out of resigning as a trustee. Fekula says little during the meeting. Later he tells me he sees the firing in terms of personality: "Donnah's a New York wise guy and Shep couldn't appreciate that."

"Donnah's capable of great work, but I didn't think we were going to get it" is all Sobel is willing to say at the meeting. Several trustees press him for a fuller explanation. "I don't want to talk here about the incidents that led up to it," Sobel answers. He agrees to give more details to any trustee who calls him, but steadfastly refuses to say any more during the meeting. The trustees are running into that immovable part of Sobel's nature: when he stands on principle, he stands fast against any amount of pressure.

The Welby incident comes at an awkward time. The Pearl's future is still at risk. Although the success of the last two shows, *As You Like It* and *Ghosts,* has lifted the bank account out of any immediate danger, fund-raising—the other half of the budget—has not kept up with the box office. The Pearl may still end the season with a deficit of thirty thousand dollars. That may well be more than Sobel and the board are willing to carry over to another season. And that would mean this is the last season of the Pearl.

Avoiding that prospect requires the board's cooperation, so

this is a particularly bad time to antagonize any of its members. It is, I realize, characteristic of Sobel to see that danger and yet not change his behavior accordingly. I've come to think you cannot completely understand this man unless you know the decade in which he came of age. In the unfailing courtesy and self-discipline with which he meets the world, Sobel often seems like a modern version of a figure at the court of Louis XIV, but in his soul he is a true child of the America of the 1960s.

🌿 APRIL 30

AIDS has not finished with the Pearl. Today Stuart Lerch tells me he has tested positive for HIV.

At the beginning of this season, the staff and company of the Pearl included five men. Their ages were thirty-two, thirty-four, thirty-eight, forty-four, and fifty-one. Now the thirty-four-year-old is dead, and two others—Stuart Lerch, who was thirty-eight, and Frank Geraci, then fifty-one—are fatally infected with the precursor HIV. I wonder how many wars kill so high a proportion of the male population in those active years of their lives.

Stuart Lerch is very tall and gaunt, with thin blond hair over a high forehead, the type who, as he says, is typically cast as an aristocrat. This season I saw him play Poseidon and Menelaus in *The Trojan Women* and Jaques in *As You Like It*. In my experience Lerch is the least outgoing member of the company, a man who will answer every question with courtesy but will never start a dialogue. He often looks as if he were off in a private world. That world has seemed melancholy to me, and today I learn why.

Lerch has just informed Sobel that though he wants to stay in the company he will play no roles in the coming season. He hasn't told anyone at the Pearl about his illness, not, however, because of its nature. "If it were leukemia I wouldn't tell anyone either," he says. "That's the way we are in my family. What's personal is personal." He hasn't discussed his illness with Frank Geraci. "We're not friends offstage, we're professionals together," he says, and he carefully adds: "Not that there's any enmity there." Nor does he discuss it with his friends outside the Pearl. What he's saying sounds familiar. "You must be WASP," I suggest. That brings the ghost of a chuckle to his melancholy voice, and he murmurs: "Super-WASP." Giving up the season at the Pearl was a "very tough decision" about what he'll do with the rest of his life. By Lerch's calculation, that life will not be long: "I assume I was infected in 1985. They say the average life span from infection is ten or eleven years. That takes me to '95, '96. But it could happen tomorrow. Or it could be '97." His deep voice is calm and resigned.

At this stage, health insurance is all-important to him. Lerch has a full-time job working a word processor at a law firm. The insurance that comes with that job covers 100 percent of the thousands of dollars he spends annually on doctors and medications. Acting at the Pearl amounts to another full-time job. "I've been carrying two full-time jobs for five years and I can't do it any longer," he says. "I barely got through this year." What's made the difficult impossible is the Pearl's move up to Off Broadway and the change from six to eight performances a week. At the same time, the law firm increased Lerch's hours in that job. "I could probably make it on the old schedule, but not now. The Pearl is growing, but I can't take that next step with them. It's frustrating. I've been very depressed these days." For the first time I hear a tremor in Lerch's deep voice, and I remember the day he said of what the Pearl means to him: "I don't ever want to lose my family.

"I had to choose one job or the other. If my health were fine I'd drop the straight job and act full-time, no question. I'd work at the Pearl six months and free-lance the other six and I'd get by. But now the biggest thing in my life is the psychology of illness. I have to drop the stage to make my life as free of stress as possible. HIV weakens the immune system, and so does stress.

I'm taking medication to try to protect my immune system. I have to reduce stress to help my body fight disease. It's an economic decision. If I give up acting, I've got a secure job, the rent's always paid, no money worries, no stress." He sighs deeply. "The flip side of that coin is that I'm a much happier person when I'm acting."

My mind goes back to our first conversation more than a year ago. We were sitting in a small Italian luncheonette in the Village. "I've wanted to be an actor since I was thirteen," Lerch said then. "I never wanted to be anything but an actor." He always felt more complete when he was someone else, he'd said, "because there isn't enough" Stuart Lerch. Now, when I remind him of that conversation, he says: "I've used the stage as an escape. I'm happiest sitting home reading and playing with my cat. I haven't married and had children. I haven't created a world that's identifiably Stuart Lerch. Ask people about me, and they'll say: 'Stuart Lerch? Pearl Theatre, that's where he works.' They don't have much more to say about me."

Looking back to his adolescence, when he started acting, he recalls: "I threw myself into it completely. It's just the age when people find out who they are. I retreated into a world of make-believe people instead of finding myself in relation to other people. Only now in my dotage am I realizing that maybe I played the cards wrong." He pauses for another long silence. "I'm looking forward to not being an actor so I can work on my personal life, of which I have very little. I want to go out and find out who I am in relation to real people."

Lerch says he hasn't been sick since he was diagnosed as HIV-positive except for an episode of shingles which he attributes to the disease. His medications often leave him tired, and twice he has been depressed enough to take drugs for it for a short time. "I've been through denial and anger," he says when I ask about the stages of the disease. "I'm now at the end of the period of action. I've got my ducks in a row. The next stage is finding more emotional and psychological support. I've always been a loner, a person who had the strength and the will to carry on by himself. That's not helping me through this, so I've had to go outside myself for help. I'm joining a support group called Body Positive. We get together and hold and pat each other and tell each other we're all right. We exchange news. There's always new information coming out about HIV." Lerch said that with his spare time—the time he'll no longer spend acting—he plans to do volunteer work and "go to museums, do all those things I never had time for."

Suddenly he says almost in anger: "I could have gone the other way. Shep would have helped me get in the Equity health plan, and there's other kinds of help available. I could almost do it, but I couldn't quite. I always said I'd die in the gutter before I gave up acting but now I'm doing the opposite. They say actors are children, and I've got to be an adult. My major concern now is the end. Dying is incredibly expensive. I don't want my family to have to be faced with that." Lerch is an army brat whose parents live in the Virginia suburbs of Washington, D.C. I ask if they know about his illness. "Yes, and they've been dreamboats about it. I couldn't ask for more."

There's a last question I feel compelled to ask: "Do you think you'll ever go back to acting?" After a long silence Lerch sighs and says: "I hope so." I hear no conviction in his voice. I realize that in this last exchange we are both papering over the reality of what he's been telling me.

Stuart Lerch is one of three actors, along with Welby and Rathgeb, who do not expect to be playing the Pearl next season. Frank Geraci has changed his mind time and again about the Pearl. This troubled man, facing a difficult time in both his personal and his professional lives, has twice said he was leaving the Pearl, and twice decided to stay. For the other three actors who will surely be back, and who are clearly the core of the Pearl's future company, this has been an excellent season. Sobel has told them the five plays he's chosen for the coming season and they are beginning to think about what roles they may hope to play.

For Joanne Camp this has been the year she played the biggest role of her career—her Rosalind. On the day after *As You Like It* closed I'd found a dejected Camp berating herself over a failed audition and hating the process of selling herself in a market where actors are treated like a surplus commodity. She soon bounced back and won a good part in *Lips Together, Teeth Apart,* a successful play running in a theatre that pays her five times the Pearl's meagre scale. She'll work in that show till early June, when she and Sobel and about half the original company of *As You Like It* go to put it on in Abingdon, Virginia, and she will be Rosalind for the very last time.

More than most actors, Camp talks about the importance of the others on stage with her. "I want actors who provoke me," she says when I ask about her hopes for the next season. "My performance is likelier to be freer and fuller than if I have to make it all up myself." She harks back to her Medea of two years ago to say one reason she failed to get her character's hatred was that "my Jason wasn't mean enough to me." She recalls Bella Jarrett, who played Hecuba in *The Trojan Women,* as a "wonderful actress who makes me better. She gave me the person to whom I could direct my energy."

Robin Leslie Brown remembers this as the season when, thanks to four successive shows under the Pearl's new contract, acting became her profession as well as her avocation: this is the great difference between Off and Off Off Broadway. "I felt like a journeyman," she says. "It was more work than pleasure, but not in a bad way. It was the recognition of the day-to-day getting up to be an actor, not glamorously being an actor. It was, I've got to go to bed, I can't go out with my friends, and for them it was, We don't see her anymore, she's always working. It's reality, not romance." Brown's voice over the phone is low and often taut, and as I listen to its characteristic sound I imagine her billowing black hair and intense blue eyes. She turns to the difference between two of her directors. "Bob Brink [who directed her in

Ghosts] is bright and he works hard, but he doesn't go in much for exploring the play with the actors. Shep, on the other hand, is big on exploration. His shortcoming is in communicating with the actors."

Like the other members of the company Brown is highly critical of her own work. (In fact, I cannot recall a single instance in which I've heard a Pearl actor speak unreservedly well of his or her own performance.) When I ask about the roles she's played this year, she immediately turns to what she considers her failure in the Chekhov farce *The Bear*. "We never succeeded at it. There were chemistry problems between me and the other actors, me and the character, more problems than there were solutions. So it never quite got off the ground." She says she regrets the loss of three members of the company, but she makes it clear she won't let it get in her own way: "That's not my job. I'm not here to be a member of anyone's family. God gave me the ability to act, and that's the job I'm here to do."

For Arnie Burton the season in which he turned thirty-three has been the best of his professional life. "I've earned more in other years, but artistically this has been my most fulfilling season," Burton tells me by phone from Houston, where he is playing in *The Baltimore Waltz* at the Alley Theatre.

Earlier in the year he'd told me he was living on a bare-bones budget so he could get by on the Pearl's pay, but still had to devote occasional Mondays off to painting or cleaning apartments to pad his income. He says he's now making a living by acting. He worked the first four shows at the Pearl, seven months during which he was earning $180 most weeks and an extra $50 a week for twelve weeks of back-to-back, when he was rehearsing one show while playing another. After *Ghosts* closed on March 14, Burton went on to *The Baltimore Waltz* at the Circle Rep in New York and now in Houston. When the play finishes its Houston run, Burton will join the Pearl's production of *As You Like It* in Abingdon, Virginia. During those four months Burton will have been earning two to four times what the Pearl is able to pay him, and he says he is saving a good portion of his pay. "Shep told me I'll probably be doing the first two shows next year," he tells me. "With what I'm saving now, that'll take me through to December without moonlighting. Then I'll go on unemployment if I can't get work." That's more than six months away, an unusual degree of job security in the uncertain world of stage acting.

Burton achieved another, more profound kind of security this year. He came to believe in himself as an actor. During our first conversation he'd told me that in his hard years he'd lost his professional way by trying to please casting directors and agents, those he hoped would get him work. In playing auditions to please others, Burton said, he'd lost his one sure asset: his unique view of the role. "I was giving away pieces of myself," he said then. Now Burton says he's learned to trust his instincts. It happened, he says, while he was playing four progressively more difficult roles. "In *Ghosts* I was intimidated for a while by the emotional life of Oswald [the syphilitic son]. I wondered, Do I have the emotional depth for this tonight—or any night? I'd push the panic button when I felt obligated to reach a certain emotional level. But when I believed I had it in me, in my own life, then it came to me. I was relaxed, I was confident, I connected to the other actors. I listened to my inner voice and let it all come out."

Their illness has pushed the Pearl's two HIV-positive actors in opposite directions. Whereas Stuart Lerch has quit acting to protect his health, Frank Geraci is seeking every opportunity to appear on stage—even if he has to hire himself, as he did for the one-man show he is now performing two nights a week.

Geraci's compelling need to practice his profession explains, I now see, the extraordinary gyrations in his relations with Sobel and the Pearl. In January, after their unhappy experience in *Tartuffe*, both men were heartily fed up with each other. Then, on March 4, Claude Underwood collapsed on the Pearl's stage during rehearsal and died the next day. Geraci, the old trouper and good soldier, came to the rescue. He replaced Underwood in the Chekhov plays. Soon after that, and somewhat to Geraci's surprise, Sobel offered him membership in next season's company. Much to *my* surprise, Geraci accepted.

"Frank's show made me see him in a different perspective," Sobel told me. "It offered me insights into how he functions, and it reminded me of what a wonderful performer he is. We were in a locked-horns position in *Tartuffe*. I'm not going to change his behavior patterns, so why get mad? If I cast him carefully, I can find a way to use his advantages and not fight what won't change. I wouldn't cast him again as Orgon, for example, at least not for the kind of Orgon I wanted. I was setting us both up for failure." He thought a moment. "I'm too stuck in the groove of, How do I make each of these actors a better actor? That's what we have to do, but we have to temper it with a sense of the possible."

For Geraci, the appeal of Pearl membership is what it has always been: the opportunity to play great roles. Sobel has scheduled *Othello* for next season, and "The chance to play Iago— whee! It's for pearls like this"—he chuckles—"that I stay at the Pearl." He says his relations with Sobel have improved while he's been acting in the Chekhov plays. "I'd do Iago even if Shep's directing it," he adds. In their tangled relations, going back now eight years, Geraci has a way of seeing Sobel, who is seven years younger, as the father against whom he once was in rebellion. "A lot of Shep is my father saying to me, 'Don't do this,' 'Don't do that.' " Geraci's hopes for the fall were quickly dashed. Within two weeks after Sobel informed the company about the next season's plays he also told them he'd cast one role already—Iago. He cast the part with an eye to the future. Instead of the veteran Geraci, a natural for the role, Sobel chose the innocent-looking Arnie Burton, twenty years younger, for whom Iago will be a stretch indeed. The disappointed Geraci came full circle again and told me he did not expect to act at the Pearl next year. "I don't see any roles I want. Shep and I have come to a time when less is more. It's best to distance myself." (But that decision would hold only briefly. Two weeks later, driven by the need to perform, he accepted two roles in next year's plays, one being a lesser part in the *Othello* in which he'd hoped to play Iago.)

Geraci's one-man show has taken the place of Seattle in his future. The night Janice and I attended the show the theatre was about two-thirds full and many of those present seemed to be friends or relatives; Geraci says the "Geraci males," including his father, have signaled their acceptance of him by coming to see him perform. Geraci appears on stage with two musicians. In his gray beard he looks older than his fifty-two years. He tells much of his story in a series of songs that he delivers in a pleasant and professional voice. It starts with his Sicilian great-grandfather's arrival in Brooklyn just a century ago. He tells about a boy who was small and out of step with his Italian family. As a teenager he took the subway to Manhattan—"the city," they called it in his neighborhood—and found himself, in every way, in Washington Square Park. He came home that day and told his mother: "I think I'm queer." He moves quickly over the intervening years to come to his present plight. He does not name his disease but no one familiar with gay life can fail to realize he is suffering from the first stage of AIDS. He brings out three teddy bears to represent three lovers. One is dead. All are gone from his life. Geraci ends his story as he began it—alone.

As Geraci sees it, this staging of his show is only the beginning. "It's a child, it has a life of its own," he says. He has arranged to videotape the show and plans a version that will include part of that tape. He intends to rework the show and take it around the country. "I want to be out there on the road singing and telling stories," he says. "There's enough in this material to keep me busy for ten years." He gives a rueful laugh: ten years is as long as he can expect to live.

Above, Michael Levin as Pastor Manders with Mrs. Helen Alving, the tormented protagonist of Ibsen's Ghosts, *portrayed by April Shawhan. Below, the Pearl's set for* Ghosts—*Mrs. Alving's house in nineteenth-century western Norway.*

Robin Leslie Brown played six roles in four shows during the season. Above, she is Regina Engstrand in Ghosts, *with Arnie Burton as Oswald Alving. In the next show,* Chekhov Very Funny, *an evening of one-act comedies, Brown played two roles. Opposite top, she is a self-dramatizing widow in* The Bear, *with Frank Geraci as her servant Louka; opposite bottom, in* The Marriage Proposal, *she is the unmarriageable daughter, with Geraci as her father. Earlier in the season, Brown portrayed the goddess Athene as well as Helen of Troy in* The Trojan Women.

Above, Dan Daily as the comic lecturer Ivan Ivanovich Niuhin in Chekhov's Concerning the Injuriousness of Tobacco. *Below, Frank Geraci in* Swan Song *as an actor at the end of his career.*

◌ MAY 6

The last show played its last performance four days ago. That Saturday night a crew of about a dozen struck the last set, the interior of a Russian summer villa that housed Chekhov's four one-act comedies. Some parts of some sets can be recycled, but not this one: the pieces of Chekhov's dismembered villa vanished into the trash. (Of the season's sets only the vines and leaves of Shakespeare's Forest of Arden will be fully preserved. The forest is packed away in boxes for Sobel to drive by rented truck to Virginia for next month's production of *As You Like It*.)

Now Sobel and Mary Harpster, aided by an occasional volunteer, are getting the theatre ready for its summer tenants. They are clearing the Pearl's movable possessions out of the ground floor and storing them upstairs or on the upper shelves of the dressing rooms. The tenants will get the lobby, the theatre, the backstage area; for the summer the Pearl's three-person staff will retreat to its upstairs office. (Larry Auld, the fund-raiser, is the third person.)

As she does every spring, Mary Harpster has been lining up tenants for the three summer months from now till the first rehearsal of next season in early August. It's a valuable contribution to the budget. At $1,600 a week, the summer rentals can add $20,000 to the year's income. Harpster has rented all the available time except the first two weeks and the week of July 4, which she says she's never succeeded in filling.

The Pearl's four tenants are a sampling of the great variety of people in this city who are seeking a career on the stage. A one-woman cabaret act will play for four weeks. She'll be followed by a group of young actors who are taking the theatre for a week to showcase themselves. "It happens quite often,"

Harpster tells me. "Some young people just out of acting school pool their resources to hire a space, invite everyone they can think of, and put on a show in the hope that someone will notice them." The summer's last tenant, the Royston Theatre Company, is a small new company that intends to specialize in classics—another Pearl, perhaps, in the making.

This evening Sobel and I are sitting in his apartment five blocks from the theatre. "It seems strange to be home on a Wednesday night," he muses. "I can't remember the last time it happened." He is slouched on a sofa sipping Scotch; it's the first time I've seen him drink anything harder than a glass of wine. "I feel like Scotch tonight," he says with a touch of defiance. This man who is usually so alert now looks exhausted: it's been a hard nine months since the August day he opened the theatre for the first rehearsal of *Tartuffe.* In the inevitable letdown after the last closing, when the stage is silent, and players and audience alike are gone, it is hard to celebrate even when the news is good.

Yet it is a time for celebration, for this was by far the Pearl's most successful season. In those nine months, it is now clear, Sobel and the trustees won their make-or-break gamble on moving the Pearl from Off Off to Off Broadway. They staked their theatre's existence on the move, and they did it, moreover, in a recession year when most small theatres saw their attendance decline, and many went out of business. "It's easier to take the measurables first," Sobel begins when I ask him to review the results of the season. The most impressive measurable is this: "More people saw our least-attended show this year than saw any show in our first seven years." The Pearl came close to the ambitious if not impossible goal of doubling its audience: it sold 13,222 tickets compared to last year's 7,348.

The Pearl is also succeeding in its financial leap forward, though not quite according to plan. The budget was supposed to balance at $380,580 (up from last season's $251,000). In the dark days of early January, before the good news from the box office and the foundations, that goal seemed far beyond reach. As of January 14, income totaled only $242,441. Even Mary Harpster's "optimistic" projection of $372,000 fell short of the budget. Her pessimistic projection of $308,000, had it come to pass, would have spelled the failure of the leap forward and, almost certainly, the end of the Pearl Theatre. It didn't come to that pass. What's happened instead is that the books are close to balancing at a lower level. In the latter part of the season, Sobel and Harpster clipped expenses where possible to try to match their reduced income. When, for example, Sobel decided to direct the Chekhov plays himself, the Pearl saved the director's fee of $1,500. A series of such small savings added up to almost $17,000. According to the figures Harpster compiled yesterday, expenses now total $363,656, and income $354,918. That leaves a deficit of $8,738—a manageable amount.

The deficit may be further reduced or even eliminated by a benefit coming up next week. The last-minute idea came from Ken Rotman, the president of the Pearl's board, and was planned mainly by a dynamic new trustee, Dr. Patricia Allen, an East Side gynecologist. It is intended to trade on Joanne Camp's presence in the cast of the hit comedy *Lips Together, Teeth Apart*. After a planning meeting at the untheatrical hour of 7:30 a.m., Ken Rotman negotiated a discount price for a block of 130 seats, which the trustees and a group of people suggested by Dr. Allen are now selling at $125 a head. For that, you get to see the show at the Lucille Lortel Theatre on Christopher Street, followed by "savories, sweets, and champagne in a turn-of-the-century town house at 45 Bedford Street, a *short* walk from the theatre," and a $75 tax deduction. As of today, the benefit is netting about $4,000. (The benefit would end up netting $8,200. After a few last-minute gains and losses, the figures added up to a deficit of only $5,000. The Pearl will go into next season in better fiscal shape than ever before.)

Change is frequent at small theatres, and often it is painful. This season at the Pearl is no exception. Some familiar faces will be missing next year. While the theatre grows, the company is getting smaller. Only three of the seven active members of this year's acting company seem likely to be part of the Pearl's future.

Of the twenty-two members of the original company only two or three—Joanne Camp and Robin Leslie Brown, and perhaps Frank Geraci—will be around next year. (Anna Minot, also an original member, is in semiretirement.) When we talked about it two weeks earlier, Sobel was unhappy: "Eight years ago I believed we had twenty-two actors who with experience and training could hold their own in a classical company. It was not so. It's shaking my foundations that the company has become so small. How can you even call it a company?" Tonight, however, he sees the size of the company in a different perspective: "We had to get lean before we could grow more muscle. It happens to every theatre with a resident company. The numbers go up and down without any relation to the success of the theatre. When I was at the Folger in Washington, everyone was talking about the Arena Stage because its company was getting so small. But the Arena Stage was actually doing very well, and in time its company grew again."

Still, a shrinking company means that the Pearl is getting no closer to Sobel's goal of a troupe of actors experienced in all the styles of classical performance. When, for example, Sobel talks of the experience "we" gained in playing Molière by staging *Tartuffe,* that "we" is primarily restricted to himself and the two or three actors who will still be in the company, though some of the others might come back to the Pearl for another Molière. Even so, he does not plan to add to the company right now. "This season proved that we can attract better people than we could before. I'm quite excited about some of the jobbers," he says, and as he speaks I see the faces and forms and gestures of those talented outsiders who flashed like comets through the Pearl's orbit. "I hope to see some of the same faces back, but adding to the company is a slower process." He stops to pour himself more Scotch, and chuckles at my look of surprise. "On the other hand, I'm not too sure where they're going to come from. I sometimes think there aren't a lot of actors out there able and willing to do this work." He shrugs, and gazes into his glass with a downcast air. "I begin to feel like the dodo bird, threatened with extinc-

tion. I must have missed the seventies and the eighties completely," says this child of the 1960s. "From all sides I get the
message 'I'd love to play Hamlet, but I've got a chance to
audition for a commercial that might pay two or three thousand
and of course I can't pass that up.'"

When I press him about whether his dream company is any
closer, he answers by talking about the progress made by the
three actors who will be around next year. "Arnie [Burton]
made big leaps, especially in speech. Also he's physically clearer.
It's not Arnie's stance, not who I am, it's who I'm creating myself
to be. Wearing period costume helps—you fill your costume.
And Joanne and Robin both made strides this year. There's the
core." When, dissatisfied, I repeat the question, Sobel is silent for
a long time. Finally he says, and now I'm hearing the artistic
director who measures himself and his theatre against a standard
set on Mount Olympus: "Well, I'll tell you. We did *Merchant of
Venice* eight years ago and nobody got it right except by accident.
This year we did *As You Like It* and we got it about half right."

Barbara Bell, the costume designer, is another Pearl veteran
who will not be back. She'll be sorely missed. Even if Sobel finds
someone as talented as Bell willing to work that hard for that
little pay, it will be a long time before a new designer can echo
Bell's statement: "I know these bodies! I know what works on
them and what doesn't." Bell told me her reasons for leaving in
her usual direct manner: "I'm a free-lancer. I need to be working
elsewhere. I can't get other work because the Pearl takes all my
time. Shep's not bringing in enough outside directors for me to
work with." Bell explained that a designer depends on directors
to ask for her services; a traveling director will typically tell the
producer which designer he wants to do his costumes. The long
hours and the commuting from her upstate home added up to
too much for too little. "I was taking home $587 every three
weeks. Shep considers that a living wage. I don't." After an
interval she said with seeming reluctance: "There were personal
factors involved. Tensions were getting high, we were at each
other's throats. I have to get out before I kill someone." I got the

impression that the longer week and longer season greatly heightened the pressures under which the Pearl people worked.

The Pearl may lose someone else at least as important as Barbara Bell to the strain of the longer season. Mary Harpster is thinking of leaving after five years here. As general manager, Harpster is Sobel's administrative alter ego. Her quiet presence often goes unnoticed, just as she slips across the stage without disturbing rehearsal, but Harpster's hand on the tiller is often what steers the Pearl away from shipwreck. Now she feels herself burning out. "Six long days a week, sometimes seven, and a season that lasts two more months, it's just too much," she says. She'd considered leaving at the end of last season, but she stayed around to be part of the great leap forward. There's another reason she may leave. Harpster and her actor husband are looking toward those pieces of the American Dream that are not part of the reality of life at the Pearl. "Bruce and I are thinking about a home and children," she says, "and that means I need more money and shorter hours."

Still another casualty of the season is the Pearl's brunch series. The brunches were part of what attracted me to this theatre: I thought I would like people who thought it worthwhile to bring actors and audiences together to talk about the play they had experienced. Now the brunches have been killed by an outbreak of human nature. It happened at the brunch for *As You Like It*. "This woman came at me when I was just arriving," Robin Leslie Brown recalled. "She said she wanted to tell me why my interpretation of Celia was totally wrong. I told her I didn't think that was what the brunch was for, and besides I hadn't even gotten my coffee, but she wouldn't lay off." The woman took her attack on Brown's Celia to the rest of those present, tempers flared around the room, and the resulting scene was so unpleasant that none of the two dozen people there signed up for the next brunch, which had to be canceled. In retrospect, Sobel blames himself for not intervening to get the discussion under control. He hopes to revive the idea next year in a different format.

Our conversation turns to the season ahead and to *Othello*. Sobel has wanted to do the play for years, but he never thought he could attract a good enough actor for the role. Black actors have few opportunities to play Shakespeare and therefore lack practice in that difficult diction; those who can do it may not want to play Off Off Broadway. But, thought Sobel, the Pearl's new status might change that. To test that belief, to see who might be interested, he held preliminary auditions in March. One day I watched half a dozen actors audition, with a young friend of Sobel's reading Iago's lines. Sobel sat in a middle row, to the right of the aisle, behind his big homemade stage manager's desk. Joanne Camp was across the aisle with a notebook. I sat behind her hoping to eavesdrop on her notes. I realized that in my mind's eye I had an image of whom I expected to see— someone who looks like Paul Robeson. As it turned out, he was the third actor to audition. The first one came and went without, as far as I could tell, attracting much interest. He was followed by a big, very dark man with a booming voice that filled the theatre. He could certainly be Othello, I thought, but I couldn't understand his reading. Then came an actor who reminded me of Robeson the moment he entered the theatre; later I was told he had actually played Robeson, though not Othello. I found myself hoping he would read well. His diction sounded clear, and I was glad to see, when I peeked over Camp's shoulder, that she'd written "excellent." I was left wondering if he would return for the real audition later in the summer.

Next year's menu looks more adventurous than this season's selections. "We're making our long-threatened entrance into the twentieth century," Sobel says of the play that will open the season: O'Neill's *A Moon for the Misbegotten*. That self-mocking line isn't strictly true—the Pearl did two new plays years ago—but this will be its first modern classic, the first one written on this side of the great watershed year of 1914. O'Neill and *Othello* are the only names as familiar as those of this year. *Othello* will be followed by Goldsmith's *The Good-Natur'd Man*, because Sobel has been wanting to do an eighteenth-century comedy, then

Racine's *Phaedra*. Sobel would like to do a Racine play every other season. He believes Racine's austere tragedies are "incredibly underrated" and wants to stage him in part for what the company can learn from the experience. Racine's plays are notable for their "economy of language and movement—you should be able to count the number of gestures. He couldn't be simpler and he couldn't be more subtle and more sophisticated," Sobel says. "If you can do Racine, you've learned economy for everything else you do." The Pearl will wind up the year with Shaw's first play, *Widowers' Houses*.

The Pearl has to keep growing to stay alive, Sobel says, and that means more money. Before long it will mean a lot more money, but not this coming year. The budget for the next season is $415,688. That's up from this year's budget of $380,580 (and actual income of about $365,000) but it's nowhere near as big an increase as this year's great leap forward. It's a budget that, with a choice of plays with smaller casts, will enable the Pearl to pay actors about $225 a week instead of $180 ("slightly less ridiculous pay," Sobel would call it). The budget will allow Sobel to offer a somewhat better fee, $2,000, to visiting directors who won't come to the Pearl for the present fee of $1,500, for about six weeks' work. The theatre suffered this season, he believes, when he had to direct three shows because he couldn't find outside directors he liked. He was stretched too thin. "The artistic director has to be the sole source of an awful lot of judgments," he says, "and he's not making them very well if it's before or after the rehearsal of a show he's directing." Already Sobel has found directors for next year's first three shows, including the black director Clinton Turner Davis for *Othello*. If his plans work out, Sobel will direct only *Phaedra*, in which Joanne Camp will play the title role.

Looking beyond the coming season, the Pearl's seventy-two-seat house cannot bring in the box-office income it will need to survive on Off Broadway. That takes a larger theatre, and that means fund-raising on a different scale. The Pearl had planned a capital campaign this year to raise $2 million for a new home, but that idea died with Ivan Polley. Sobel and Ken Rotman agree that the present trustees are unlikely to raise that kind of money. "Our board is wonderful, but they don't play in that league," Sobel tells me. "It doesn't start with an application to a foundation. It starts with a serious talk with someone who can write a check for $250,000. We're beginning to know such people. We're a bit closer to the overnight success it will seem when someone pulls out a checkbook and says, 'Look, here's one-third of the cost. Put my mother's name on your new theatre.' " Of this person, Rotman says: "We probably know him, we just don't know which one he is—or she."

Sobel makes a sudden gesture, almost of anger, and sits up straight on the couch. "I have to be very careful at this stage," he says in an earnest tone unusual for him. "My job could easily become chief fund-raiser. We have to remember that our mission is not to get bigger, it's to do better work." He makes a questioning motion with his hand. "How do you measure success? It's so tempting to go by what you can measure. 'We made forty thousand'—great, that we can count. But did *The Trojan Women* affect people? Who knows! If the success of the corporation ever becomes our first priority we'll have sold out our original charter. We'll only be successful. We won't be important." When I ask him whether he thinks *The Trojan Women*—the play that gave me my most memorable experience of the season—*did* affect people, he says: "When you do that play you're taking on an enormous responsibility to the gods of the theatre. We did some good things there, we affected people to some degree, but not deeply enough. The audience shouldn't even be able to get up after it! They should have to go to the recovery room, not the restaurant. We didn't quite achieve that." Remembering my own response to the play, and substituting the restaurant's bar for the recovery room, I suggest to Sobel that he's never satisfied. To my surprise, he manages to find danger lurking in that possibility: "The trap is to say it's an impossible goal. I didn't pull off *The Trojan Women* but then who ever does? At least I tried! It doesn't serve the work to think like that. I just want to raise what I'm willing to settle for—because what you'll settle for is what you get."

I'm reminded of a story Stanislavski told about the early days of his theatre. They'd gone on tour to St. Petersburg. Late on the night before the opening Stanislavski saw out his window people standing on line in the bitter winter cold. He realized the people out there were waiting for tickets to his production, and he thought: "My God, what a responsibility we have to satisfy the spiritual needs of these people who have been standing here freezing all night. What great ideas and thoughts we must bring to them! So consider well, whether we have the right to settle accounts with them by merely telling them a funny anecdote. I could not fall asleep that night for a long time because of my feeling of responsibility. I felt the people whom I had seen in the square deserved much more than we had prepared for them." Stanislavski's story helps me appreciate Sobel's sometimes exasperating insistence that a performance that's only good enough isn't good enough for him, that his actors must never aspire to be less than great, and that nothing in their lives or his own matters compared to what happens on the stage. Sobel, I now see, wants a theatre that stages performances for which we'd gladly stand out in the cold of a Russian winter night.

Sobel yawns. His eyelids are drooping and he's slouching down on the sofa again. "It's been a difficult year," he murmurs. "I'm battling burnout." His spirits soon revive, and then he tells me more clearly than he ever has why he does what he does and what reward it gives him: "I have a notion of what I want the Pearl to do in theatre. What happened this year is that my theory got confirmed—that what I want to do is a very good thing to do. It may be lofty, but it's a legitimate goal, and it's an important one. At the end of this year I believe even more firmly in the importance of theatre than I did before. Theatre is not a luxury, it's an essential, it's a cure. It's one of the indicators that you have a solid, vital society going. I'm more sure than ever that I should be doing what I want to be doing. That's a great feeling. I doubt that a whole lot of people get to feel that way about their lives."

We sit in a companionable silence. Sobel looks at his watch and exclaims: "Quarter of eleven! Joanne'll be home soon." He excuses himself to "do a couple of things" before his wife returns from her evening performance. I am left to reflect on what I've just heard. The thought comes to me that what unites the people I've been spending the past year with is that, in their separate ways and to varying degrees, they all believe with Sobel that they should be doing what they want to be doing, and that it is indeed a great feeling. I see images of enthralling moments I experienced this year in that small theatre, and I recall what Patricia Allen said when asked why she wanted to join the Pearl's board: "My life and the lives of my children have been transformed by our experiences at the Pearl. I want to transform the life of the Pearl." Theatre at its best transforms us by enabling us to live other lives without actually suffering the consequences. When, at the close of *The Trojan Women,* Hecuba says: "Forward:/into the slave's life," we feel ourselves go into slavery with her, yet we walk out of the theatre free men and women. That experience, it seems to me, comes close to defining us as human beings; and that sense of our own humanity is what the actors and their ground crew offer us—surely it must be "a great feeling" to be doing such work!

The silence lengthens while my thoughts drift over the years that led me to this moment, the decades since our great Russian visitor entertained a five-year-old boy with his clothespin moustache, down to these enchanted months that I have spent with his descendants. The lives of actors are far harder and more uncertain than my own; right now, however, I find myself envying them the magic that inhabits them at the moment of creation. A sense of unease, of not belonging, comes over me as I sit alone in that living room, and I realize, with a reluctance that surprises me, that the story I came for has ended. My season with the Pearl is over. It's time for me to leave.

David Hapgood was born and grew up in New York, and graduated from Swarthmore College. He has been an editor and writer for *The New York Times* and was a Fellow of the Institute of Current World Affairs in West Africa. Mr. Hapgood is the author or co-author of *The Murder of Napoleon, The Screwing of the Average Man, Monte Cassino,* and *Africa from Independence to Tomorrow.* He has also been a translator and an evaluator for the Peace Corps. He lives with his wife, Janice, in New York.

A NOTE ON THE TYPE

This book was set in a version of Monotype Baskerville, the antecedent of which was a typeface designed by John Baskerville (1706–1775). Baskerville, a writing master in Birmingham, England, began experimenting in about 1750 with type design and punch cutting. His first book, published in 1757 and set throughout in his new types, was a Virgil in royal quarto. It was followed by other famous editions from his press. Baskerville's types, which are distinctive and elegant in design, were forerunners of what we know today as the "modern" group of typefaces.

Composed by ComCom, a division of
Haddon Craftsmen, Allentown, Pennsylvania
Printed and bound by Arcata Graphics/Martinsburg,
Martinsburg, West Virginia
Designed by Anthea Lingeman

MOLIÈRE'S TARTUFFE

SEPTEMBER 6, 1991 THROUGH OCTOBER 19, 1991 (P) = Preview Performance

MON	TUES	WED	THUR	FRI	SAT	SUN
				6 (P)8pm	7 (P)5pm (P)9pm	8 (P)2pm
9	10 (P)8pm	11 (P)8pm	12 7pm GALA	13 8pm	14 5pm 9pm	15 2pm
16 8pm	17 8pm	18 8pm	19 8pm	20 8pm	21 5pm 9pm	22 2pm
23 8pm	24 8pm	25 8pm	26 8pm	27 8pm	28 5pm 9pm	29 2pm
30 8pm	1 8pm	2 8pm	3 8pm	4 8pm		

NON-SUBSCRIPTION DATES
Tues 10/8,8pm – Wed 10/9,8pm – Thur 10/10,8pm – Fri 10/11,8pm – Sat 10/12,5pm&9pm – Sun
Tues 10/15,8pm – Wed 10/16,8pm – Thur 10/17,8pm – Fri 10/18,8pm – Sat 10/19,5pm&9pm

EURIPIDES' THE TROJAN WOMEN

OCTOBER 25, 1991 THROUGH DECEMBER 7, 1991 (P) = Preview Performance

MON	TUES	WED	THUR	FRI	SAT	SUN
28	29 (P)8pm	30 (P)8pm	31 7pm GALA	25 (P)8pm	26 (P)5pm (P)9pm	27 (P)
4 8pm	5 8pm	6 8pm	1 8pm	8pm	2 5pm 9pm	
11 8pm	12 8pm	13 8pm	14 8pm	9 8pm	9 5pm 9pm	10 2p
18 8pm	19 8pm	20 8pm	21 8pm	15 8pm	16 5pm 9pm	17 2p
				22 8pm	23 5pm 9pm	24

NON-SUBSCRIPTION DATES
Mon 11/25,8pm – Tues 11/26,8pm – Wed 11/27,8pm – Fri 11/29,8pm – Sat 11/30,5pm&9pm – Sun 12/1,2p
Tues 12/3,8pm – Wed 12/4,8pm – Thur 12/5,8pm – Fri 12/6,8pm – Sat 12/7, 5pm&9pm

SHAKESPEARE'S AS YOU LIKE IT

DECEMBER 13, 1991 THROUGH JANUARY 25, 1992 (P) = Preview Performance

MON	TUES	WED	THUR	FRI	SAT	SUN
16	17 (P)8pm	18 (P)8pm	19 7pm GALA	13 (P)8pm	14 (P)5pm (P)9pm	15 (P)2pm
23 8pm	24 8pm	25 8pm	28 2pm 8pm	20 8pm	21 5pm 9pm	22 2pm
30 8pm	31 8pm	1 8pm	9 8pm	27 8pm	28 5pm 9pm	29 2pm
6 8pm	7 8pm	8 8pm	10 8pm	3 8pm	4 5pm 9pm	5 2pm
					11 5pm 9pm	12

NON-SUBSCRIPTION DATES
Tues 1/14,8pm – Wed 1/15,8pm – Thur 1/16,8pm – Fri 1/17,8pm – Sat 1/18,5pm&9pm – Sun 1/19,2pm
Tues 1/21,8pm – Wed 1/22,8pm – Thur 1/23,8pm – Fri 1/24,8pm – Sat 1/25,5pm&9pm

IBSEN'S GHOSTS

JANUARY 31, 1992 THROUGH MARCH 14, 1992 (P) = Preview Performance

MON	TUES	WED	THUR	FRI	SAT	SUN
3	4 (P)8pm	5 (P)8pm	6 7pm GALA	31 (P)8pm	1 (P)5pm (P)9pm	2 (P)2pm
10 8pm	11 8pm	12 8pm	13 8pm	7 8pm	8 5pm 9pm	9 2pm
17 8pm	18 8pm	19 8pm	20 8pm	14 8pm	15 5pm 9pm	16 2pm
24 8pm	25 8pm	26 8pm	27 8pm	21 8pm	22 5pm 9pm	23 2pm
				28 8pm	29 5pm 9pm	

NON-SUBSCRIPTION DATES
Tues 3/3,8pm – Wed 3/4,8pm – Thur 3/5,8pm – Fri 3/6,8pm – Sat 3/7,5pm&9pm – Sun 3/8,2pm
Tues 3/10,8pm – Wed 3/11,8pm – Thur 3/12,8pm – Fri 3/13,8pm – Sat 3/14,5pm&9pm

CHEKHOV'S CHEKHOV VERY FUNNY

MARCH 20, 1992 THROUGH MAY 2, 1992 (P) = Preview Performance

MON	TUES	WED	THUR	FRI	SAT	SUN
23	24 (P)8pm	25 (P)8pm	26 7pm GALA	20 (P)8pm	21 (P)5pm (P)9pm	22 (P)2pm
30 8pm	31 8pm	1 8pm	2 8pm	27 8pm	28 5pm 9pm	29 2pm
6 8pm	7 8pm	8 8pm	9 8pm	4 8pm	5 5pm 9pm	3 2pm
13 8pm	14 8pm	15 8pm	16 8pm	10 8pm	11 5pm 9pm	19 2pm
				18 8pm		

NON-SUBSCRIPTION DATES
Tues 4/21,8pm – Wed 4/22,8pm – Thur 4/23,8pm – Fri 4/24,8pm – Sat 4/25,5pm&9pm – Sun 1/26,2pm
Tues 4/29,8pm – Wed 4/29,8pm – Thur 4/30,8pm – Fri 5/1,8pm – Sat 5/2,5pm&9pm

| SEPTEMBER | JANUARY | FEBRUARY | MARCH | APRIL |